MAKING A WORLD OF DIFFERENCE:

Liberation from dehumanization, alienation and stress in the market-driven society

NADJA U. PRAETORIUS

Copyright ©2017 Nadja U. Praetorius
All rights reserved

The right of Nadja U. Praetorius to be identified as author of this work has been asserted by her in accordance with the Copyright, Designers and Patents Act, 1988.
No paragraph or illustration of this publication may be reproduced, copied or transmitted without written permission from the publisher in accordance with the provision of the Copyright Act 1956 (as amended).

This book is sold subject to the condition that it shall not by way of trade or otherwise be lent, resold, hired out or otherwise circulated without the publisher's prior consent in any form of binding or cover other than that in which it is published, including this condition being imposed upon the subsequent purchaser.

ISBN 9788792632852
Second edition, in English
First edition 2016 isbn 9788771298994 published in Danish by Klim, Denmark

published by Whyte Tracks, Denmark

TABLE OF CONTENTS

FOREWORD..8
DEDICATION AND ACKNOWLEDGEMENTS........................9
INTRODUCTION..11
   Brief outline of the contents..12
      The book is divided into two parts......................................12

PART I   REFLECTION UPON THE MODERN
             WAY OF LIFE...15

CHAPTER 1   ANOTHER PERSPECTIVE.................................17
   A timeless moment in space..18
   An age of change and new departures....................................19
      The Japanese disaster as an emblem..................................21
   Evolution and technological development:
   a contemporary paradox? 22
      Who is connected?..24
      Rational bypassing...27
      Qualified optimism..29
   Participation and intervention..30
      The unveiling of deceptions...32
      An indication of turning points?...33
      Challenges to change..35
      The cost of neglecting the human factor 37
      The existential choice...39

CHAPTER 2   THE VITAL ABILITY TO REFELCT AND
             INVESTIGATE 41
  A crack in time 42
    Interpretations of reality 43
    Selective Distrust 44
    Fixed mental structures and neural networks 45
    Reflection and investigation 46
    Is humanity losing its influence? 48
    Reality deprivation 49
    The human involvement 51
    Existential choices 53
  Theories about humanity 54
    Quantitative research methodologies 55
    Qualitative research methodologies 56
    Methodological considerations 57
    Rational bypassing and Complementarity 59
  Humanity in an all-embracing perspective 60
    The complex human being 61
    The rediscovery of direct experience 62
    The gracious space of compassion 63

CHAPTER 3   THE SIGNIFICANCE OF MEANING 65
  The overlooked subject 66
    Normative assumptions and scientific incapacitation 69
    Crazy or normal? 70
    Consequences of scientific lapses 72
    Georg's forest 73
    Reality converted into language games 74
    The unruly reality 75
    The responsibility for basic sanity 75
  The existential point of departure 76
    Basic human preconditions 77

Meaning, coherence, perspective, and value 78
Making sense of meaning 80
The need for value, appreciation and belonging 82
The survival strategies of powerlessness 82
Existence, meaning and ethics 83
Counteracting the dire consequences of
reductionism and reification 84

CHAPTER 4 ALIENATION, STRESS AND CONFORMIST
INDIVIDUALISM 85
Out of the box – out of the closet? 85
A metaphor: 86
The alienated human being 89
    Alienation and inner homelessness 90
    The fragile identity formation of alienation 91
    The relation between dehumanization, alienation,
    and stress 92
    Self-perpetuating estrangement 95
    Depression and stress 96
    The work-adjusted concept of competition 97
    Competition, truth and deceit 99
    The normalization of untruthfulness 100
    Prescribed untrustworthiness 102
    A case on untrustworthiness 103
    When untrustworthiness hits home 105
    When reality has to be redefined in order
    to be endured 107
Conformist individualism 108
Research with the telescope to the blind eye 110
    When scientific status is bestowed on urban legends 111
    Emancipation from the hegemony of
    dehumanization and alienation 112

PART II EXPLORING THE HUMAN POTENTIAL 115

CHAPTER 5   DEVELOPMENT: EMPATHIC COOPERATION OR
             ALIENATING SUBMISSION? 117
  The wonder of the unpredictable 117
    Perspectives on childrearing in a Polynesian Island 118
    Blind spots and eye openers 122
  Groundbreaking research on the human processes
  of formation 123
  Attachment theories 127
    Attachment, exploration, and empathy 128
    Attachment over time 130
    Attentive empathy and rational manageability 130
  Being and development 134
    Survival strategies and inner estrangement 135
    Alienation and traumatization in the personality formation 137
    Personal emancipation as maturation process 138
  The societally relevant human being 140
  The ethical challenge of our time 141

CHAPTER 6   IN PURSUIT OF THE AUTHENTIC 143
  Who do we want to be? 143
    Individuation – Independence – Authenticity 144
    The ethical dilemma of the individual 145
    Who do we think we are? 146
    What do we mean by "evolution"? 147
  An indigenous culture 150
    What good are questions? 152
    A different life 155
    Glimpses of change 160
    The same, yet incomparable 161

CHAPTER 7　LANGUAGE AND THE MULTIFACETED
　　　　　　REALITY 163
　Language, identity and the all-encompassing reality 163
　　Reflections on language 166
　　Questions we refrain from asking 169
　What we can learn from Mungiki 170
　　Communal sharing and caring 171
　　Taupongi's journey 172

CHAPTER 8　SEEING THE EXTRAORDINARY IN THE
　　　　　　ORDINARY 175
　Dream and reality 175
　　The imperceptible self-forgetfulness 177
　The unification of supposedly irreconcilable aspects 178
　　The Ethical Paradox and Existential Considerations 179
　　Different causes for the separation 182
　　The ethical paradox and biological preconditions 184
　　The common ground of the existential and the biological
　　perspectives 186
　　Overcoming the battle of survival: an account 186
　　The ethical paradox on a societal level 187
　Paradigm shift: investigating reality 189
　　Exploration of the multi-faceted mind 191
　　Seeing the extraordinary in the ordinary 193

Bibliography 195
About the Author 205

FOREWORD

Never before has such all-encompassing research been carried out and nor has the disciplinary specialization been greater. Nadja U. Praetorius is rare in that she combines findings from diverse fields. But if the application of knowledge is truly to benefit humanity, this is the only way forward. Praetorius draws on everything from anthropological and psychological, to physicists' and zoologists' studies, in order to address the crippling concept of humankind as presented by an economically driven society, including the way our children are socialized.

Today a capitalist market economy prevails. Restrictions on global trade have been lifted; production, trade and transportation have created wealth, but have also caused a growing inequality amongst humanity, and harm to the climate and the global environment. On a national level, governmental economic authorities are dominant in relation to the departments that deal with the environment, education, social conditions as well as cultural areas.

Marketization penetrates ever deeper into what was previously the private sphere and traditional caregivers such as family structure and local social networks are on the retreat. "Networking" in this day and age is carried out often cynically motivated, to gain an edge on the competition and managerial thought on manipulating others has reached new heights. Praetorius shows how today, our goals for future development supplant our sense of presence in the here and now.

The current market economy mindset is built on a primitive ideolgoy of self-interest and maximization that causes alienation of the individual and creates scores of mental and physical afflictions. Paradoxically, we are becoming individualized - in a conformist manner.

Nadja U. Praetorius sets the stage for a much-needed revolt against the dominance of this misconception of humankind. In a masterful stroke, she revives the almost forgotten concept of 'alienation'; at state whereby having the natural connection with our inner selves, and our human potential stifled, we become alienated. Then the possibility of entering into anything more than merely manipulative relations with others, is diminished.

Nadja U. Praetorius wishes to return authenticity to humankind, so we all can lead full lives, instead of being crippled conformist individuals. Her book deserves a wide circulation.

Tim Knudsen
Professor emeritus of political science, Department of
Political Science, University of Copenhagen.

DEDICATION AND ACKNOWLEDGEMENTS

MAKING AWORLD OF DIFFERENCE is a compilation of and renewed reflection on my past 17 years of research and scientific articles, my previous books and chapters in anthologies, as well as my clinical experience. An update and revision of knowledge, experiences and insights about conditions of which I have had a growing understanding over the years. This is not least due to meeting with people I have supervised individually or in their workplaces and educational institutions. People that I have held numerous presentations for in meetings and conferences and who has generously shared their experiences with me. People who like myself live in an ever-changing world with a growing sense of being deprived of influence. People who want to devote themselves in creating together with others a transition to decent and sustainable conditions for all - recognizing that we have all that it takes to do so.

MAKING A WORLD OF DIFFERENCE derives from a collective movement, brought about by countless known and unknown people. A movement that, with ever greater power and clarity, insists on claiming our human right to stand by and express unique and undeniable human qualities. A movement that grows out of the certainty acquired in contact with what is perceived as truth, elevated over debate.

It is with humility and gratitude that I dedicate the book to human beings who, in the history of humanity have contributed to this movement and to those who all over the world now and in the future, have a deepfelt wish to contribute to this movement.

To me personally, the people in my life - my family and friends - are invaluable in their genuine interest and support of my preoccupation with the concerns dealt with in the book. They are a constant inspiration in my life and work.

The first English translation of the Danish version of the book was made by my son, Samuel Ben Israel. Later, the translator, Dan Marmorstein edited the text, so it now appears in a very fine English version. I am grateful to both of them for the excellent result.

Helle and Ib Foder, Bolette Nyrup and Svend V. Loldrup are my collaborators in an initial effort to bring ethics and a deeper understanding of the nature of man to the agenda in a broader public. They have spent many hours studying the Danish edition of the book. Their comments and insights have been extremely useful, and their enthusiasm in the joint project has been contagious and encouraging. In all phases of the writing of the book I had the good fortune of receiving enthusiastic support from my good friends and colleges, Birgitte Nørbo and Malene Friis Andersen. For that I am deeply grateful. Apart from reading and commenting on the book's manuscript, they have engaged with me in lively, and from time to time heated, but always mutually insightful discussions about the work that for all of us occupies so much of our awareness, lives and hearts.

My teacher H.E. Mindrolling Jetsün Khandro Rinpoche's ever-present clarity, life-giving inspiration and caring compassion is a daily reminder that it is humanly possible and profoundly meaningful to think and act for the benefit not only for ourselves but for everyone else with whom we share our living conditions. That it is in moments of self-forgetful presence, in mutual exchange of indestructible human qualities, that we in our daily lives experience the unique - the extraordinary in the ordinary.

INTRODUCTION

MAKING A WORLD OF DIFFERENCE highlights the necessity of liberating humanity from the incapacitating dehumanization and alienation of the current market society. It also presents the breaking of new ground in our understanding and appreciation of who we are and what we can actually accomplish as human beings.

The diminishment and alienation caused by organizational and management procedures that are aimed at maximizing efficiency and productivity in workplaces and educational institutions, has led to an unprecedented increase in physical and mental disorders. Being a cross-cultural scientist and clinical psychologist treating patients with work-related stress, anxiety and depression I feel urged to bear witness to how the regime of standardization, control, evaluation and competition is a serious threat to the mental and physical health of citizens in the marked societies all over the world.

The transformation needed at all levels of society in order to create globally sustainable living conditions depends on the active cooperation and participation of citizens who will stand up for and realize the very humanitarian values and attitudes, that in our current market societies are being neglected, intimidated, and suppressed.

Thus, the socioeconomic dogma that competition between people, social institutions and nations is necessary in order to survive is about to cut off humankind from their unique human capacities and natural urge to cooperate in communities and express empathy and a rich variation of human qualities and values.

MAKING A WORLD OF DIFFERENCE is a profound call to renewed reflection and action. The analysis and descriptions of our current condition offered by the book are based on contemporary studies within the political, social, and natural sciences, combined with psychological and neurobiological research and clinical observations. The conditions in workplaces and in educational institutions described in the case studies and accounts throughout the book demonstrate that todays all too common psychological imbalances such as depression, anxiety, and traumatic stress are human reactions to inhuman conditions.

Readers are furthermore invited to reflect upon age-old human wisdom, on various philosophical and spiritual parables, and on accounts from a field study that I carried out in an isolated Polynesian Island. The book is an inquiry into the reality that we share and which we more or less consciously and sometimes willingly, sometimes against our will, are creating together. It is my hope that the book can serve as a mirror in which we can clearly recognize the significance of being human and thereby be inspired into renewed reflection, consideration and transforming action.

Brief outline of the contents

The book is divided into two parts.

Part I.: The central theme of Part I is the analysis and documentation of the subtle but ever-more intrusive totalitarian ethics upon citizens in our contemporary democratic market societies. A reliable presentation of the current situation is vital if we want to bring to an end, the disempowering management procedures that threaten to alienate us from contact with our own unique human qualities. A disempowerment that prevents us from living as free and healthy people, concerned with the wellbeing of ourselves as well as that of other human beings.

It is well documented that management strategies based on fear and distrust make us uncertain of our own worth and personal judgment leaving us in an impotent state wherein we are likely to surrender to external control and manipulation. It is also documented that the loss of both personal integrity and the certainty that comes from being true to ourselves, has fatal consequences in the form of alienation, stress and disease. This results in not only immense financial and human costs, but also constitutes a tremendous democratic problem. At the community level one can fear that the disempowered, alienated and stress-ridden citizens increasingly feel isolated and powerless and without the necessary capacity to cooperate in communities and in the democratic processes and contribute to the necessary transformation into sustainability at all levels in society.

Part II.: The consequences of a number of historically and culturally limiting conceptions of man and of our reality which prevents us from exploring, nurturing and developing our full potential as human beings, leads us in Part II to the other main theme of the book ie: the (re)discovery of ourselves as human beings. A breaking of new ground in our understanding and appreciation of the nature of humankind is reflected upon, and investigations are undertaken in order to see if this can halt the current trend towards individualism and focus on self-interest. A new departure, which may contribute toward a realization that we exist in a multi-dimensional world of inter-connectedness where the values and qualities each of us unfold with the intention of benefiting others, and will inevitably also benefit ourselves.

This realization could be the natural ethical basis in meeting the challenges of our time, and may prove to be a golden opportunity for us to break with historical, devaluing notions of who we are as human beings. Taking decisive steps towards a more comprehensive manifestation of who we are is a starting point for the creation of a reality and a world that is beneficial to ourselves and the Earth we share with all living beings. Acknowledging that it is a matter of survival of all, or of none.

PART I.
REFLECTION UPON THE MODERN WAY OF LIFE

CHAPTER 1
ANOTHER PERSPECTIVE

"...And I believe that if the world is going to change for the better, something must change first of all in human consciousness, in the humanity of contemporary mankind; mankind must somehow come into its own; must free itself from the awful entanglement of all apparent and hidden totalitarian mechanisms, from the all-consuming repression of advertising and media manipulation, must rebel against being a gratuitous part of a giant machine directed God knows where, humanity must regain for itself, a deeper responsibility for the world - which means an accountability for something higher than one's self."

Vaclav Havel (1936 -2011)[1]

The courage that characterized Vaclav Havel's life, his art and active opposition towards all kinds of totalitarian repression, was rooted in his conviction that it is humanly possible not only to reveal, and refuse to give in to one's contemporary conditions, but also to take responsibility for reconsidering and transcending identification with degrading and distorted perceptions of who we are as people. In his writing and talks and with his life at stake, he participated with like-minded people in the liberation of his country from the dictatorial communist regime's blatant repression. But he did not stop there. As is apparent from the quotation, the discovery of totalitarian trends and our responsibility not to submit to them, became for him, a lifelong concern.

The search for and exploration into the (re) discovery of something that is felt to be original and uniquely human, has occurred in all cultures throughout the history of humanity. Especially in difficult times, the folktales, myths and parables of philosophical and spiritual wisdom schools have been told and retold with the intention of shedding light on this reality in which we find ourselves. A light that not only shows our reality as we commonly perceive it, but also encourages us to see the situation from a different, more comprehensive perspective. The stories express a human universal wisdom to remind us that we are anything but pow-

---
[1] Havel, 1991 The quote is derived from the Danish edition of Havel's book, and translated into English.

erless. And on the contrary, these stories urge us to wake up from our man-made nightmare and reconsider our predicament. The fables not only talk about how wrong things can go, but also delve into deeper layers of our minds where we are moved by the recollection of something profound in our existence and stirs memories of indestructible human qualities, that we have either forgotten, been indifferent to, or rejected because we were attracted by something that seemed more promising and alluring.

This chapter takes as its point of departure a contemporary event which - like the folk tales from the past - introduced a whole generation in the last century into seeing reality from a different, timeless perspective. An event, leading to potential reflection and reconsideration of how we want to see ourselves as human beings and our fellow human beings, as stewards of everything we share with all life on Earth.

A timeless moment in space

> When the first images of Earth as seen from space were distributed to news outlets around the world, Earth was dubbed the "the blue planet." Together with these images, we received the astronauts' accounts of the moment, when they for the very first time were able to observe Earth from an entirely new perspective. The breathless feeling of seeing something so familiar and mundane, floating brilliantly and blue within the infinity of space, was presented with an almost solemn humbleness and awe in a moment's recognition of something magnificent beyond all imagination and conceptualization.

> As a truly universal, existential testimony, the accounts of the astronauts were dispatched around the world along with the images of the blue planet.

> Soon, the images could be seen everywhere, on posters in schools and homes, on book covers and stamps. Regardless of the purpose of travelling into space, the images and the existential reflections of the astronauts were pivotal to our perception of Earth as incredibly precious. Seeing Earth and our existence on the planet in this perspective nurtured an appreciation of what a privilege it is to regard Earth as the basis of our lives and similarly served to remind us that taking care of the Earth and protecting it falls to the lot of mankind.

The images portrayed an almost ethereal beauty and made Earth appear very different from other depictions we hitherto had created in the form of maps and globes. There was an inherently natural and pristine ambience to Earth. From that perspective, any notion that it is pierced by borders or that vast areas belong to some and not to others, in turn causing conflicts and wars between tiny people crisscrossing the planet, seemed absurd and meaningless.

We embraced the images of the blue planet as a daily reminder from space. The images left us with an incipient awareness that Earth was given to humans, animals and plants as a communal habitat, where life unfolds in a myriad of relations of interaction, exchange, and mutual interdependence.

The image of Earth became an icon of the incipient awareness that inspired the organization of the first peace and environmental movements. It came to symbolize an ancient realization that we need, from time to time, to see things from a higher and more comprehensive perspective in order to catch sight of what's right there in front of us.

Seeing the images of the blue planet for the first time in history constituted a turning point in our self-perception and that of the world. Not because we learned more about space but because we were given an opportunity to learn more about ourselves and to reconsider life on Earth.

An age of change and new departures

The age we live in is marked by change and new departures. Some claim that we have just witnessed the beginning of a future that we can hardly imagine. In a more pessimistic vein, others doubt that we have the courage to do so.

A fortnight after the earthquake off the coast of Japan on March 11, 2011 and the subsequent tsunami and the havoc that ensued at the Fukushima Dai-ichi I nuclear power plant, the Japanese Prime Minister Naoto Kan stated that all efforts were being made to prevent a worsening of this very grave situation. He added: "We are not in a position where we can be optimistic." It is hardly possible to imagine a more ominous statement, let alone one that was issued by a Japanese prime minister who, in his wording, was complying with the traditions of a culture where emotional and disturbing statements are considered offensive by the recipients of the message.

Naoto Kan's statement to the Japanese public – as well as to the rest of us – came at a time when the disaster was proliferating, day by day and minute by minute, with ripple-like effects and expanding into an increasingly serious situation of unanticipated magnitude. This was a time of having to face an impossible situation while attempting to stem the escalating tide of deterioration. The solutions devised and implemented proved eventually to be counterproductive and harmful – both in the short and the long term – as soon as they were drawn up and put into use. The impossibility of the situation also manifested itself in the question of how long it could be endured by those designated to work in the disaster area – seeing that they were facing a constant danger to their very lives and really ought not be there – while, at the same time if they were relieved of their tasks, nothing else could be done to prevent a progressive worsening of the situation.

As the threefold disaster of earthquake, tsunami, and damage to the nuclear facility lost its newsworthiness for those of us who are not living at the actual site, our worst fears about the far-reaching consequences of the disaster gradually became a concrete reality. Information was being conveyed slowly, drop-by-drop and became progressively more alarming when the real scale of the damage was publicized – revealing a damage that to this day is apparently still manifesting in uncontrollable ways.[2]

A meltdown of the reactors *did* happen, with extensive radioactive pollution, not just in the power plant's immediate surroundings but also spread out over a far greater area than had been initially indicated. The pollution affected not only the land but also the air and the sea. As more and more information comes to light, it becomes increasingly clear what immense harm we are dealing with. Currently, the long-term effects of the catastrophe are estimated to last half a century.

The cleanup after the tsunami and the nuclear disaster along with the reconstruction of homes and infrastructure for thousands of Japanese people, as well as the attempts to resuscitate the partly paralyzed industrial production, altogether predictably flung the world's third largest economy into a recession, with consequences reaching far beyond Japan and the Japanese society. The consequences of the meltdown at the Fukushima Dai-ichi I nuclear power plant, as documented by the International Atomic Energy Agency, are still, as of this writing, evolving and spreading to areas farther and farther away from Japan.

---

2 For updates on the long-term effects of the nuclear disaster, see: International Atomic Energy Agency http://www.iaea.org/newscenter/focus/fukushima/

The Japanese disaster as an emblem

Can the disaster in Japan be said to be emblematic of the groundwork we have laid with the immense economic and technological development and growth of the post-war years, and can it also be an example of what we could expect in the future?

Could it be that the global economic crisis which has shaken the politico-economic makeup of society since 2008, with its various apparently unforeseen catastrophic effects, be perceived as a parallel disaster to the earthquake in Japan? The only difference being that the Japanese "occurrence" appears far more concretely intelligible and almost simple, from an external viewpoint? Does the catastrophe stand forth as some kind of "objective lesson" about the far-reaching and unintended consequences of economic growth and technological development brought about because the possibility presented itself? [3]

During the past 30-40 years, it has become increasingly clear that economic growth and technological development, regardless of the increased material wealth for many, has proven to have far-reaching adverse consequences in the form of the exhaustion of Earth's resources, in pollution, climate changes and threat to all life on the planet. In addition to this, there are very real human costs. Exposed to the dehumanizing and alienating demands of a market society that reaches for ever greater efficiency and productivity, an alarming number of people present mental and physical imbalances and illnesses of a magnitude that has not been witnessed before.

The question is whether we can expect momentous changes in the time to come, changes owing to, for instance, man-made or natural disasters, recurring financial crises and collapses, or threats and attacks against the present social order from new powerful forces, both domestically and globally, with consequences that we can hardly imagine. No one can answer this question with any certainty but more and more people are inclined toward venturing a qualified guess that *anything is possible*.

An international team of scientists, mathematicians and philosophers at Oxford University's *Future of Humanity Institute* is presently investigating the most importune dangers to the survival of life on Earth. There is a general consensus that we are living in the first century of Earth's history where the greatest threat to the survival of life on the planet comes from humanity. In a research paper [4], the director of the institute,

---
3 Meadows et al., 1972.
4 Bostrom, 2012

professor of philosophy **Nick Bostrom**, states that we have entered a new kind of technological era with the capacity to threaten our future as never before. These are threats that we have no track record of surviving. Likening this to putting a dangerous weapon in the hands of a child, Bostrom argues that the advance of technology has overtaken our capacity to control the possible consequences.

The hitherto dominant incentive for growth and development - that is, competition and the greatest possible gain for individuals as well as for businesses and countries – seems to have become counterproductive, to an increasing extent, in a globalized world: a world in which it has become increasingly clear that we are all mutually dependent on each other and where it seems all the more relevant to focus on developing our uniquely human capacity to cooperate.

Already now, it may prove crucial that we, individually and collectively, as citizens in democratic societies and as co-creators of the world, stand ready and willing to reflect upon the following questions:

1. What will the handling of current crises and the prevention of coming disasters demand of us?

2. What will it take for us to deal with the extensive changes that we are going to have to accept?

3. How can we, as human beings, muster what it takes to create completely new and sustainable conditions for life in a global era?

These questions are essential for the themes of the book and will be dealt with throughout the book.

Evolution and technological development: a contemporary paradox?

In the following, light will be shed on contemporary paradoxes that need to be considered in order to avert counterproductive tendencies of our time.

The products of technological development – having simultaneously assisted science and having come into being through science – have become everyday commodities and have in the space of a few decades turned everyday life upside down and drastically changed the way we communicate with and relate to each other. Uniquely human capacities for thinking and reflection, for being creative and innovative, and for producing knowledge that far exceed our ordinary capacities of comprehension all underlie the scientific and technological breakthroughs of our age.

Due to the paradigm shift within physics in the previous century, our ideas and concepts about the material world as being comprised by clearly defined, fixed, and immutable objects located in relatively predictable, three-dimensional space have been supplemented and even supplanted to some extent by a multidimensional understanding of reality. In these dimensions of reality, time, space, and causality interact and are transcended in paradoxical and apparently inexplicable, unpredictable ways, just as the very act of observation hereof influences and is influenced by the observed.

Phenomena of reality, thus, cannot exclusively be grasped by rational and conceptual thought but may, in some cases, be approximated and rendered probable on the basis of, for instance, mathematical calculations that are in turn verified experimentally. At the same time, the continued development of new approaches to gaining knowledge and expanding understanding has affected a wide range of research fields. Mathematical methods developed within the natural sciences have thus been applied in disciplines like economics and social sciences.

It is quite remarkable that we have become so familiar with incredibly complex matters that are crucial to the technological and scientific advances which shape our daily lives while, at the same time, our knowledge of the human mind and our unique ability to think and reflect, to be intuitive and creative – the precondition for all this to appear and manifest – is relatively limited and that the human nature and the human mind remains so unexplored. Furthermore, if we consider the notion of humanity that underlies the domineering socioeconomic ideology and its technology based management approach it becomes evident, that we are facing a contemporary paradox: On the one hand, we uphold the assumption that the technological development, product creation and management approaches bear witness to a progression in the human evolution. On the other hand our contemporary socioeconomic ideology takes its point of departure in a notion of humanity, asserting that our way of thinking and feeling and our attitudes towards ourselves, our fellow human beings and our environment are regulated by primitive drives and survival instincts that assigns us a position at the level of animals. A notion of humanity that – as will be shown later – is influenced by popular interpretations of Darwinism and Freudianism.

The question is whether these simplified notions about humanity – that underlies the socioeconomic and technological management practices - function as self-fulfilling prophecies. That we in other words not only are prevented from unfolding our full potential but that we – by subordinating to the management practices – gradually accept to identify with the grotesque reduced notion of humanity.

These considerations give rise to reflections on whether adherence to a reduced and obsolete notion of humanity contributes to the assumption that we - as stated by Nick Brostrom and other researchers – have not currently matured our human potentials and values to the degree that we are able to handle the technological development appropriately. We will return to this issue later. First, in the following sections some mundane examples will be given of how modern technology especially in the last 15-20 years, has increasingly occupied a central position in our everyday life.

Who is connected?
The ideas and motives that lie at the root of the extraordinary discoveries that led to the development of our highly advanced information society were supposedly fairly simple and transparent from the outset: 1) to relieve people of burdensome tasks, which were taken over by machines; 2) to streamline workflow and production in order to secure the greatest possible product outcome and profit. A continual development of software ensures that computerized management and organization set up the framework for and monitor a wide range of both private and public work tasks, with the manifest aim of increasing growth in production and effectiveness of workplace performance.

In the course of technological development, however, it is often the case that completely new agendas are to be found in the very processes of developing and applying technology. The invention and development of computer technology and the Internet serve as textbook examples of how shifting agendas take over, condition and control not only the use of technology but also, at times, the people for whom the technological tools were originally intended as aids.

In the course of the development of computer technology and with the advent of computers in workplaces and within the education milieu, shifts in the perspective of the computer technology's use have continually occurred. Right now, it seems that people are increasingly perceived as the computer's collaborator – sometimes as the boss, other times as the employee but, in any event, always subjected to the software's organization, project management, standardization, control and assessment.

Even though particular motives, purposes or intelligence cannot be attributed to technology in itself, it is hard to conceal the fact that there has been an imperceptible shift in the basic view of humanity in the course of the process. We will take a closer look at this in Chapter 4, "Alienation, Stress and Conformist Individualism". The politico-economic pillars of the market society – streamlining, productivity, growth and competition – support a management mentality that is based on a view of humanity which constitutes a perfect fit to the ongoing development of computerized management technologies. This has, to a great extent, transformed human capacity and identity into an interchangeable commodity, which is continually being adjusted to fit into and conform to a constantly changing labor market.[5]

A single example can serve to illustrate how an altered view of humanity can imperceptibly be integrated in the individual's perception of self and reality and simultaneously sow the seeds for a change of language. The diffusion of the Internet and the revolutionary significance it has acquired, not only in the labor market but also in the rapidly marginalized private sphere, illustrates this. Computers were originally stationary and mostly tools of the workplace. At the time that the Internet was introduced, we spoke about computers being connected to the Internet. As stationary computers found their way into our homes, we could also connect the computer at home to the Internet. After laptops came to replace stationary computers and especially after the explosive dissemination of tablets and smartphones, we became carriers of computerized technology ourselves. We no longer say that my tablet or smartphone is connected but rather that I am connected. And since my portable devices have their regular place in my pocket or my bag and because the Internet connection is secured practically everywhere in the public domain, my connection is no longer conditioned by time and place: whether I find myself in a work context or am off-duty, I am always connected. With the advent of computer technology in daily life and its gradual takeover of everyday communication-functions and transactions between people, one could get the impression that we – without realizing it – are becoming appendages to the technology we are the carriers of.[6] For better

---
5 Praetorius, 2002; Akerlof & Kranton, 2010
6 Turkle, 2011

or worse, we are becoming dependent on – and becoming increasingly addicted to – the gratification of being updated at all times.

No one wants to be regarded as a simple-minded Luddite. Fortunately though, remembering and enjoying comedy's invigorating illustrations is still feasible. For example, Charlie Chaplin's undying movie, *Modern Times*, which, if anything, confronts us with the perspectives of being connected to machines and with other consequences of technological progress. Presently, computerized robots that are capable of taking care of the disabled and of elderly people – for instance, during the consumption of daily meals – are being programmed and tested. Reviewing the scene in which Chaplin, as the factory worker, is strapped to a food machine, so that the consumption of his lunch will not adversely affect productivity, may give rise to second thoughts. Perhaps this was Chaplin's anticipation of what today is called "Lean Management", where, in the name of efficiency, the phasing-out of human presence and mutual relations between people is actively being carried out within ever more expanded areas of the workplace. If this gets carried to its extreme, it could mean that encounters between doctors, social workers and teachers, on the one side, and those who are being cared for, helped or taught, on the other, will become a matter of instrumental efficiency. In the process, mutually nourishing relationships are being reduced and impoverished, resulting in the alienation of both parties, who are left with a sense of having been rendered redundant as human beings. [7]

The great importance ascribed to technological progress and the attempts to optimize efficiency in the workplace seem not only to be based on but have also contributed to an altered view of humanity. This has transpired without much notice – and it would be tempting to say "behind the backs" of the general public.

During the same period as these radical changes took place, learning and developmental processes have chiefly been found interesting when they are viewed in the light of political recommendations and when the priorities of business and industry are taken into consideration. The emphasis has particularly been placed on how human potential can be exploited to the benefit of productivity and the growth of economic prosperity. Perhaps it is precisely due to this absence of a more comprehensive knowledge about humanity that it becomes increasingly uncer-

---

[7] An account of the lifelong need for attachment with others in order to experience oneself and function as a human being will be given in Chapter 5, in connection with the presentation of attachment theory

tain whether we can put our trust in renewed attempts to create further growth in production and consumption.

Rational bypassing

To understand this, we have to consider some historically and culturally determined omissions that occurred at the time of the advent of Enlightenment, some four hundred years ago, when a shift of perspective in the perception of life and reality was introduced. This led to the emancipation from religious dogma and doctrine and curtailed the powerful hegemony of the church over individual life and thought. For many centuries, this hegemony had prevented innovation within philosophy, art and science. The new departure had a crucial impact on the norms and standards that were subsequently established in science and paved the way for the industrial revolution. Thinking based on reason and rational argument gained ground, to the detriment of the introspective and intuitive way of developing knowledge. Subjective, qualitative observation – linked to the religious and metaphysical realms – lost its legitimacy to the objective and predominantly quantitative way of exploring, recording and obtaining information about reality. Hence, a split emerged in the view of the human mind; thus, a subjective and apparently amorphous, unmanageable irrational entity was contrasted to an objective and rational intellect. This dichotomy eventually laid the ground for a binary way of thinking that discounted the human capacity to mobilize and utilize a large number of subjective categories of experience, whereby we are able to sense, have insight into and understand the multidimensional nature of mind and reality.

Today, we attach crucial importance to our knowledge about the phenomena of reality that we acquire by turning the radio telescope toward the immense vastness of space[8] and the electron microscope toward the tiniest possible specks of matter and life. We do so, not being all that concerned with the fact that we possess a uniquely human mind without which we could not grasp or do anything with the very reality we are in the process of examining, exploring, making sense of, and creating. Scientific exploration of the human mind is today, by and large, confined to the steadily growing fields of research that study the brain and the genes. Thus, research into the mind seems to occupy a secondary position in relation to the exploration of the function and capacity

---

8 In July 2015 the "Breakthrough Initiative", financed by Russian physicist and billionaire Yuri Milner in cooperation with among others the British physicist Stephen Hawking , was initiated in order to investigate if intelligent life is to be found in the Universe. This is according to Hawking the greatest question that still awaits an answer.

of the brain and of genetic dispositions that, from this perspective, are perceived as the origin and seat of mind.

What appears to be an ever more pressing question is why we apparently view the human mind from a perspective that only allows a very limited and one-dimensional exploration, which cannot form any sufficient basis for a deeper and more comprehensive understanding of the mind's nature and functioning. This seems to be all the more incomprehensible when we stop and consider that scientists who are working within the realm of modern-day physics are dealing, apparently without effort, with an external reality that ostensibly cannot be understood and described, unless theories and mathematical models are continually created that take into account the fact that the reality being examined not only appears multidimensional but also inexpressible.

It seems obvious that it is not possible to conceptualize reality as multidimensional unless the mind and our powers of cognition are characterized by a capacity to operate in a multidimensional way. A relevant topic for reflection is how this observation could benefit the way we perceive and act in the very reality we are part of and create in our daily lives. Examining this issue in depth might prove to be essential for the current situation of the world and humanity. The reason for this is that reductionist thinking about humanity and about our way of dealing with the inventions of technology is counterproductive and can potentially pose a threat to life on Earth in the foreseeable future.

"Thinking outside the box", which is so enthusiastically advocated when it comes to coping creatively with our current situation, might accordingly include relinquishing what I call "rational bypassing". Rational bypassing is the tendency to suppress some part of the capacity of our mind by means of which we are able to gain insight and knowledge that we cannot achieve by rational thought alone. Thus, 'objective' methods of exploration have dominated science at the cost of 'subjective' ways of studying, exploring and gaining knowledge and insight such as introspection, reflection, self-reflection, empathy, creativity and innovation. These latter aspects of our mental functioning can be regarded as complementary to – and mutually dependent upon – our capacity for rational thinking. In addition, we in any case constantly in our everyday use - and need to apply - these subjective ways of experiencing and realization in order to maneuver in and make sense of the reality we are part of and create with others.

It is an important point here that 'exploration' refers not only to scientific research. The human capacity to investigate and explore are preconditions for each of us to gain insight and understanding, thus creating both coherent perspective and meaning in a constantly changing reality. We are dealing with unique human skills that are inextricably linked to our ability to maneuver in life as healthy, whole, and viable people and fellow human beings. This will be described in more detail in the next chapters of the book.

Qualified optimism

Perhaps it is time for a thought experiment in which we examine the possibility of perceiving our current situation from a perspective and with an attitude that we could call qualified optimism. This qualified optimism is not to be regarded as a counterweight to a pitch-black pessimism, cynically factoring in the total breakdown and the inevitable end of life on the Earth. Neither should qualified optimism serve as an equally fatally blind optimism that is based on a denial of the exceedingly serious condition of the Earth, the biosphere, and humanity. Just as much as pessimism, such a perspective – and such an attitude – would inevitably serve to fixate us in proceeding into the impasse of powerlessness

Qualified optimism must base itself on knowledge, rational thought, a sense of understanding about – and most especially confidence in – the object of qualified optimism. This "object" cannot be anything but humanity itself. Not just because we are the ones who are responsible for our own plight and that of life on Earth, but also because humanity embodies and encompasses the very potentials, qualities and capabilities that are indispensable for dealing with the tremendous challenges we face, both now and in the future.

It is not a question of renouncing the progress that has been brought forth by economic growth and technological development. What is needed is rather a change of perspective, enabling us to make use of the very same abilities to think rationally, to be creative, and to be innovative – in order to reverse the devastating course, before it is too late.

However, a key aspect of the notion of qualified optimism is that we can trust that our handling of the challenges and the building of global, sustainable ways of life are informed by a fundamental concern for the common good. In other words, that they are informed by our ability and willingness to accept the responsibility for bringing into effect measures that will be of benefit to all living beings, and to the planet – our common basis of existence. [9]

---
9 Daly, 2009

Participation and intervention

Proponents of neoliberal market thinking apparently ascribe an innate metaphysical power and intelligence to the market and its mechanisms, which are conceptualized as dramatically surpassing humanity's ability to ensure economic stability and a fair distribution of resources. Even today, these proponents are warning against initiatives that would regulate the economy and would distribute extremely vast sums of capital through state-controlled institutions. Refraining from adopting such measures is, of course, beneficial to a more and more affluent elite, while the real income of the middle class tends to stagnate or fall. At the same time, a growing number of poorly paid or unemployed workers and employees and extremely poor people all over the world are barred from having any share in the growth, and the gap between the rich and the poor countries are increasing. [10]

A growing number of social scientists, economists, and specialists working within environmental and climate research - who are endeavoring to break free from the dominant neoliberal politico-economic thinking and practice - appear to agree on one issue: if we are going to handle the current crises and to prevent coming fatal disasters, it is imperative that we make comprehensive changes in our consciousness, in our opinions, in our values, and in our habitual ways of being and acting in the world. [11] It is held to be of the utmost importance that we individually and collectively are willing to be consciously aware of a more responsible usage and equal distribution of Earth's resources. Not sometime in the future, but right here and now.

Acknowledging the situation in which we are standing takes courage. That being said, courage does not seem to weigh heavily on powerful financial enterprises, neoliberal economists, and politicians around the world. On the contrary, being "tough as nails", taking a cynical stance and feigning ignorance continue to inform their thinking and acting, as if the economic crisis, the catastrophic state of the Earth and millions of people can be mollified by employing exactly the same methods that gave rise to these conditions. [12]

A new discourse in the field of political economy that dismisses the neoliberal theory and dogmas has recently been published by French economist Thomas Piketty in his groundbreaking work, *Capital in the Twenty-First Century*.[13] This highly acclaimed and best-selling book fo-

---
10 Acemoglu & Robinson, 2011; Hickel, 2012
11 Held, 2010
12 Hickel & Arsalan, 2012
13 Piketty, 2014

cuses on empirical studies of wealth- and income-inequality in Europe and the United States that have been conducted as far back as the 18th century. Piketty's central thesis is that *wealth* will accumulate if the rate of return on capital is greater than the rate of economic growth. Over the long term, Piketty argues, this will lead to the concentration of wealth and economic instability. Piketty proposes a global system of progressive tax and transfer that would help bring about greater equality and dampen the tendency for the vast majority of wealth to come under the control of a tiny minority. Piketty argues, furthermore, that unless capitalism is reformed, the very democratic order will be threatened.

Moreover, Piketty forecasts a world characterized by low economic growth, thereby discounting the idea that bursts of technological advances will bring growth back to the levels enjoyed during the 20th century, arguing that we should not base ourselves on the whims of technology.

The American professor of economy, David Harvey, takes the analysis a step further in his book, *Seventeen Contradictions and the End of Capitalism*[14]. For Harvey, the concentration of capital in the hands of a small economic elite already changes the government of democratic societies into oligarchies and plutocracies that are increasingly taking over the power to control not only finance and policy-making but also media and education. For Harvey, the suggestion put forth by Piketty related to increasing taxes on the exorbitant fortunes and raising the minimum wages is not going be sufficient to avoid the breakdown of capital, nature and humanity. A whole new movement that points to alternative ways of socioeconomic thinking and acting is, according to Harvey, indispensable.

In line with Piketty and Harvey are certain international initiatives to further new economic thinking relating to the worldwide economic crisis. Thus, leading economists around the world regard the dogma of the perfect market and the presumption of rational actors that has been posited by neoliberal economic theory as contributory to driving the financial crisis out of control. The Institute for New Economic Thinking (INET), led by six Nobel Prize laureates, has set out to create an alternative to neoliberal theories. In just a couple of years, INET has attracted 10,000 members. Economists and students of economy around the world are drawn to a new economic thinking and it has been reported that students are organizing protests at their respective universities, demanding that up-to-date economic theories and analyses be taught.

---

[14] Harvey, 2014

The unveiling of deceptions

Seen from an overall perspective, the most powerful deceptions of the current market society are the view of humanity and the dogma that asserts that competition on all levels of society and between nations is necessary in order to survive: a dogma that implies that survival is a matter of "us or them". It is deceitful in that it has been able to overshadow the natural urge of human beings to socialize and cooperate in communities while expressing uniquely human qualities and values.

It now seems to be high time to remember how lies and deceit have been central ingredients in the takeovers of totalitarian regimes and how new rulers have been able to hold people in the grips of a distorted reality with the application of inhuman force. Under such conditions, corrupting people all the way down in the hierarchy has been simple, with the effect that citizens partly developed a deep mistrust of others and partly had their sense of trustworthiness undermined.

It is noteworthy that the administration and governing of citizens in ways that hint at totalitarian management are still being implemented and are actually on the rise in established democratic societies. In his book from 2008, [15] the American political philosopher Sheldon Wolin illustrates what he coined " inverted totalitarianism in managed democracy", where every natural resource and every living being is commodified and exploited to the point of collapse. Wolin describes how, in managed democratic societies, the community is lulled and manipulated into surrendering their liberties and their participation in their governments through the avenues of excess consumerism and sensationalism. According to Wolin, this is especially evident wherever policy making is dominated by powerful economic enterprises. Wolin describes a country where citizens are politically apathetic and submissive – and where the elites are eager to keep them that way. At best, the nation has become a "managed democracy", where the public is shepherded and not sovereign. At worst, it is a place where corporate power no longer answers to state controls.

The American historian and political philosopher Francis Fukuyama expresses similar points of view in the recently published second volume of his major work on the evolution of the world's political institutions. In this latter volume, *Political Order and Political Decay*, [16] Fukuyama analyzes and depicts the development of liberal democracy from the French Revolution up to the present day. The prospects for democracy are, according to Fukuyama, uncertain. Taking his point of departure in the history of

---
15 Wolin, 2008
16 Fukuyama, 2014

America, Fukuyama demonstrates that the political development in America – and Europe – in the past few decades has shifted into reverse gear, as its states have become weaker, less efficient and more corrupt. Thus, growing economic inequality and the increasing concentration of wealth has allowed elites to purchase immense political power and manipulate the system in order to further their own interests. The increasing lack of participation of citizens in governing society and the all-too-prevalent tendency of human beings to be motivated by self-interest rather than by being concerned about the common good are, for Fukuyama, among the main threats to the progressive development of liberal democracy.

The Italian philosopher Paolo Flores d'Arcais also spots real threats to democracy that can be attributed to the hegemony of economic and political power that leaves citizens marginalized and powerless. It is necessary, d'Arcais argues, to radically change the paradigm of the existing democratic societies in order for the citizens to regain sovereignty as free and equal members of society who will cooperate through active participation. [17]

While reflecting upon Fukuyama's rather pessimistic notion of the limitations embedded in human nature, one is given cause to wonder whether a change of paradigm – as advocated by d'Arcais – is at all within reach. And if so, who will take upon themselves the task of preparing for and bringing about such a change?

An indication of turning points?

Perhaps it is right now that we have to realize that there is no time to waste and that we – to use a metaphor from the world of sports – are already operating in "injury time". That we – whether we like it or not – are compelled to take the necessary steps that may turn the tide decisively. To that end, we have to be willing to unveil the deceptions that tend to allure us toward passivity and submission and, at the same time, we have to be willing to reconsider what it implies to be human.

Recent initiatives might point to turning points leading toward the creation of new democratic structures and institutions, with the unprecedented participation of citizens all over the world. After the financial crises, a series of insurrections going by the name of "Stop-movements" emerged in Europe and America. These revolts can be seen as a nascent clash with an ideology of deprivation and inequality that affects a large number of people, locally and globally. These clashes with powerful financial institutions might constitute an awakening to

17 d'Arcais, 2014

the significance of radically empathizing with others instead of simply promoting one's own narrow interests.

These thoughts are presently being actualized in new networks of business-activism, where people all over the world are participating with knowledge and skills in the invention, production and sharing of commodities at less material cost and are, at the same time, creating human social communities of mutual exchange. *The Sharing Economy* or *The Collaborative Economy*, as these new economic initiatives are called, are motivated not only by the possibility of creating more and sustainable economic value, through sharing and co-creating products, but aiming as well at generating social relations and values in human communities. [18]

In his latest book, *The Zero Marginal Cost Society*, [19] Jeremy Rifkin goes so far as to predict that the capitalist era is passing and that a new global Collaborative Commons that will fundamentally transform our way of life is going to arise. Even now, hundreds of millions of people are, according to Rifkin, transferring parts of their economic lives from capitalist markets to global and networked Commons. As a result, "exchange value" in the marketplace is, according to Rifkin, increasingly being replaced by "use value" on the Collaborative Commons. In this new era, Rifkin asserts, identity is less bound to what one owns and more bound to what one shares. Rifkin concludes that while capitalism will be with us for at least the next half century, it will gradually lose its role as the dominant paradigm. We are, Rifkin says, entering a world beyond markets, where we are learning how to live together collaboratively and sustainably in an increasingly interdependent global Commons. [20]

Initiatives toward the implementation of the sharing economy and collaborative commons may be considered necessary and most welcome. They are motivated initially by humanitarian attitudes and values and they involve the participation of citizens all over the world. A fundamental change envisioned in the ideas of collaboratively and sustainably interdependent global Commons presupposes, however, people's willingness to work consciously and actively toward cultivating humanitarian values and people's willingness to be guided by motives, intellectual

---

18 An example is QuiShare, an Internet-based platform organizing initiatives and projects globally according to the concept of collaborative economy. Collaborative economy is defined as practices and business models that are based on horizontal networks and the participation of a community, transforming how we live, work and create in an age of communities.

19 Rifkin, (2014

20 The custom of sharing sustainable goods on the indigenous Polynesian island of Mungiki will be dealt with in Chapters 6 and 7 of this book.

skills and creativity that support the establishment and progressive development of these communal ways of living. In other words: setting up new structures of communication and exchange may be necessary but not sufficient. The underlying mindset and necessary skills also need to be shared and further developed by the members of such communities.

Taking part in making the changes, however, tacitly requires a willingness to be aware of what we are up against, externally, and a willingness to remain aware of what we, on a personal level, encompass with regard to qualities and to limitations, especially when it comes to realizing our intentions and wishes for change. In the following, some external and some personal challenges will be dealt with and reflected upon.

Challenges to change

With the intention of throwing a historically - and perhaps realistic - light on today's challenges in initiating a breakthrough in consciousness and view of human nature, we will take a closer look at events that took place in the century before the present.

Throughout the history of mankind, we have witnessed incomprehensible acts of cruelty and infamy as well as genuine expressions of selfless empathy, compassion, and love. The previous century has been described as the century of evil and the most violent in the history of humanity – with its world wars, its genocides and its massacres perpetrated by dictatorial regimes. A century in which human beings, by the millions, were mercilessly plundered, humiliated, and murdered all around the globe, and not just by hostile forces but also by their own dictatorial rulers and fellow countrymen.

At the same time, it was also a century where measures to prevent such atrocities were initiated. International organizations like the United Nations were established to ensure adherence to human rights and to prevent conflicts and the dictatorial use of force against humanity and to put a stop to assaults committed against millions of people around the world.

It is thus important to remind ourselves that we in the century of the great world wars and racial persecution were enriched with brilliant personalities - like Mahatma Gandhi, Martin Luther King and Nelson Mandela. Their profoundly humanitarian thoughts and actions struck a chord in people around the world who unremittingly, and in tune with humanitarian motives, worked together with others, at risk to their own lives, to alter the most miserable and humiliating conditions of life for millions of oppressed people.

Accounts of genuine heroism on the part of survivors of concentration camps, of wars, of brutal oppression brought on by dictatorial regimes, of natural disasters and of economic meltdowns, and the heroic efforts of healthcare professionals working in areas inflicted with deadly epidemic diseases move us and remind us that it is certainly possible to stand up to challenges and endure difficult times in ways that we hardly knew we ever possibly could. Their deeds serve to remind us that we are capable, when it is imperative for ourselves and for others, of getting in touch with capacities and forces within us that allow us to display insight, ingenuity, courage, will power, strength, and selfless compassion for others, regardless of whether these qualities characterized us and our way of life prior to such unbearable conditions.

The reason that we commonly tend to point to the actions of a few exceptional people in equally exceptional situations might be that we – not only in our own time but throughout the history of humanity – have ingested accounts, stories, legends and myths that allow us to mirror and recall innate qualities we all possess, jointly. Perhaps we tend to overlook and forget that we, quite naturally – and for as long as we have been living in human communities on Earth – take into consideration, in the course of our everyday lives, the welfare of others and that we display empathy, consideration and care for each other. We tend to forget that these human qualities and our ability to cooperate are among the crucial preconditions for our survival as a species on Earth. [21]

Thus, the recent years humanitarian crises brought about by the migration of refugees, and the Western, rich countries increasingly short-sighted and cynical refusal to care for people who flee from death and annihilation, seems to have aroused new popular, humanitarian movements. This also applies to the formation of spontaneous volunteer networks to support the country's own citizens that are gravely affected by financial cuts in health, social care and education.

Internet-based networking, news coverage and think tanks, are emerging to make up for the policy of oppressive political and economic systems. Common to these movements is that they consist of citizens that - in the short term - want to make themselves available and show compassion in very specific situations, and - in the longer term - want to follow their visions to create ethically-based, sustainable and empathic communities and social relations by and for the people. Communities, where freedom in creating innovation, creativity, artistic expression and a life in harmony with our natural environment is a top priority.

---

21 Mithen, 1996

The movements can be seen as an opposition to the dominant regime where citizens are kept on a tight leash by the governing and mindset of an economic and political elite and its narrow perspective of the necessity of competition and self-interest. There is, however, not simply a rebellion against the established order, but a consciousness change and transformation driven by the desire and need for a new departure in view of humanity and new lifestyles, created by and for the benefit of people.

It is easy to get the impression that we live in a constant and inevitable struggle between good and evil. That we, as human beings, are caught in a deep split and that we – so to speak – owe our very survival to people who can step in and clear up after the egoism, the greed and the destructiveness of others. To people who seek, with all their might, to prevent attacks on decent ways of living, driven by an exceptional confidence that true goodness, now and in the future, will turn out to be victorious.

The question is whether this dualistic struggle between good and evil is an indispensable condition of life, as something inevitable and essential to being human, and that we just have to hope that a sufficient number will bestir themselves the day the world falls apart.

The cost of neglecting the human factor

The question is whether we can wait until it becomes inescapable. And whether there is any point in waiting. Even though we have not suffered devastating floods and droughts in our part of the world and even though we are not the victims of war and dictatorial oppression, we are still connected to other parts of the world by mutual dependency and we are increasingly affected by what occurs there.

The most important reason, however, is that we are already – so to speak, in our own backyard –more than amply affected. Because we, in many ways, have let ourselves be seduced and alienated by exactly the way of thinking and acting that is seated at the root of the current man-made breakdowns and disasters. In an increasingly competitive market society, the measure of success for the individual and for society – nationally and globally – appears inextricably linked to the capacity to compete for the greatest possible achievement and growth for the mere sake of increase in material wealth and profits for the few. To this end, the education of the citizens of a younger age is being focused on manufacturing useful "agents" who are being measured, under the designation of "human capital", in terms of their ability to identify with and exemplify this overriding economic manner of thought.

Analyses of the neoliberal society and the underlying political-economic and social theories indicate that the pre-theoretical assumptions feature reminiscences of a kind of popular Darwinism and Freudianism. Humanity is seen as controlled by (survival) instincts and self-interest and as being driven, basically, by a hedonistic urge to achieve the gratification of needs, drives and desires in the struggle for survival. It stand to reason, then, that humanity will not, on the basis of its own free will, benefit society and the common good but rather needs to be induced – to put this in a way that juxtaposes human beings and animals – with a carrot and stick. In our competitive societies, this view of humanity is being reinforced by fear-based conditioning and by new strict management strategies and methods of control and evaluation.

This reduction of human beings – this way of cutting people off from their human potentials and values – has left clear marks. An ever-greater number of people – both domestically and globally – are suffering from physical and mental imbalances and illnesses due to the strains and dehumanization experienced on the job. This has been well documented by numerous scientific studies, among these being *WORK STRESS AND HEALTH: the Whitehall II study*, an ongoing longitudinal study including more than ten thousand British civil servants. What the Whitehall II study substantiates is that stress at work results from an imbalance between the psychological demands of the job, on the one hand, and the degree of control over one's work, on the other. It is, then, not the demands themselves that are the major cause of illness, although high demands can be linked independently with ill health. It is, more than the demands as such, the *combination* of high demands and low control. [22]

In recent years, there is increasing evidence that hazardous working conditions pose an economic threat. The International Social Security Association estimates that the economic burden of work-related injury alone is equivalent to 4 percent of the world's Gross Domestic Product (GDP) and, in some countries, as high as 10 percent of the GDP. In the United States, the annual costs of occupational injuries and disease have been calculated at $250 billion. On the other hand, there is mounting evidence of superior market performance of enterprises that nurture a climate of health and that incorporate social concerns in their sustainability efforts. It accordingly appears to be so that sustainable work and health are integral to organizational and economic sustainability. [23]

---

22 Ferrie, 2004
23 Homepage of American Psychological Association: http://www.apa.org/wsh/ . Retrieved on May 5, 2014.

The existential choice

The notion of "qualified optimism" that was introduced earlier rests on the confidence that it is possible to break free from the current alienation, regimentation and undermining of what is best in humanity. And that we – by consciously striving, even now, to clarify our outlook and reflect upon what motivates us – are increasingly ready to make choices about whether to be guided by self-interested striving in order to achieve the most for ourselves, in competition with others, or to be guided by an equally accessible and altogether natural capacity to cooperate and think and act to the benefit of both ourselves and others.

What is essential to the notion of qualified optimism is that it is just as easy to have pure motives to sustain the way we make use of our qualities and potentials as it is to be governed by, for instance, selfishness and lust for power. And that acting on behalf of the common good is liberating - and deeply meaningful.

Perhaps the greatest challenge is having the courage to see that we, potentially, are responsible: all the way from the beginning until the end. To see that we are accountable for the deceptions and distress of our time, to the extent that each and every one of us takes part in and contributes to the causal relations that constitute the backdrop for the increasing destruction of ourselves, of each other and of life on Earth. However, acknowledging that we are, in fact, co-creators of the present conditions of the world is precisely what is needed for us to liberate ourselves from a feeling of incapacity and a feeling of being victimized by the conditions that are damaging to us.

The challenge of becoming co-creators of a new departure in ethical thought and action implies that each and every one of us chooses to work consciously toward ripening and cultivating fundamental human qualities, empathy and compassion. No one can take this challenge away from us; nor can anybody take over the task for us. It is with this realization in mind as a starting point that we can make the existential choice to unfold our values and attitudes in practice – a choice that we make, knowing full well that we have to be willing to be aware not only of what we are up against, externally, but also of what each and every one of us holds, regarding both qualities and limitations, when it comes to adhering to our choices.

It may be a matter of due care and diligence to start reflecting upon whether we are presently being faced with the necessity of making an extraordinary effort in an extreme situation that is going to last until what is hopefully the impending end of the crisis or whether the changes we have to prepare for and take part in imply that we should take a long-term view and realize that nothing is going to be as it was before. This latter realization might be tantamount to a golden opportunity for us to prepare an awakening and a process of emancipation in which we, with increased clear-sightedness and awareness realize what human beings are actually able to cope with.

The main intention of this book is to elucidate the fertile ground in humanity from where we can be liberated from the rule of the competitive market society and from the perpetual strategies to secure oneself without worrying about others. Relinquishing the limited and simplified perceptions of self and of the world entails that we rise above the dehumanizing notions of who we are and reevaluate our capacity and willingness to unfold meaningful ways of being and living. This presupposes that we reclaim the capacity of the human mind to explore, to reflect upon, and to gain insight into our own potential and qualities, as well as acknowledging the beauty of life on the Planet which sustains us.

Devoting time and space to getting to know ourselves and to whatever in a deep sense gives meaning to us engenders insightful openings, where we can directly perceive and acknowledge what is – as it is – and in its own right. Where we can appreciate, in our ordinary everyday lives, the preciousness of our true being. As when we, in golden moments, realize that everything takes part in a continuous and potentially vitalizing, dynamic interaction, in an all-encompassing state of existence, in mutually interdependent relation with all there is. The way we experience this when our habitual concepts and fixed thought structures dissolve in a self-forgetting, timeless moment, and we see the extraordinary in the ordinary – like when for the first time, we saw the image from outer space of Earth, the blue planet. [24]

---

24) I learned of the phrase "Seeing the extraordinary in the ordinary" in the course of H.E. Mindrolling Jetsün Khandro Rinpoche's exposition of Longchen Rabjang's (1308-1363) comment to The Guhyagarbha Tantra during the Annual Retreat, Mindrolling Lotus Garden, 2011, USA. The phrase thus belongs to an advanced level of Buddhist philosophy, namely, the Vajrayana. In the present book, which is not a Buddhist text, it is used to express everyday events and spontaneous experiences in which conventional understanding is transcended by insight belonging to another level of knowing.

CHAPTER 2
THE VITAL ABILITY TO REFLECT AND INVESTIGATE

In this chapter, we will examine our experience of reality and investigate the preconditions for our way of relating and acting in the world.

Reflections will be made on how the precedence of the linear and one-dimensional time axis over the experience of the "space of time" as well as the tendency to deal mainly with Quantity-related measurement at the expanse of examining quality constitute a considerable limitation of humanity's field of reality. Thus, it is suggested that this entails a devaluing of humanity and a limitation of our self-perception and self-expression.

Various contemporary social theories and the underlying assumptions that they posit about human beings are presented. These theories constitute handed-down ways of thinking that we, to a greater or lesser extent, have taken for granted and with which we have identified ourselves. What is shown here is how this affects our notion of who we are as well as our way of life.

"Rational bypassing", the tendency of current science to neglect paying due consideration to direct experience and to individuals' first-person singular expressions, is brought into focus. It is discussed how this reinforces collectively shared and alienating views of reality. The human proclivity to make use of a wide range of subjective categories of experience is a precondition for thinking, reflection, self-reflection, empathy, creativity and innovation, the very competences that are needed most in the process of emancipation from reifying views of humanity and in the creation of new visions and conditions for human life on Earth.

The chapter starts and ends with encounters I had while I wrote the chapter. Encounters that became significant for writing the chapter.

A crack in time

The loudspeakers inside the commuter train play an announcement for the passengers. On this Sunday morning, it is aimed at those of us who are just about to get off the train at Nørreport Station in downtown Copenhagen: "Keep an eye on your belongings and remember to take them with you when you leave the train," it declares.

At that very moment a man – clearly marked by not just the previous night but by years of amply sampling various liquid substances – walks, with firm steps, toward the exit while proclaiming, in a loud and clear voice: "Keep an eye out for YOU. With regard to your belongings, we can work that out." Moments later, he has disappeared into the crowd.

What is actually going on in the split second that the loudspeakers' announcement, based on an apparently factual rendering of reality, is brought into confrontation with the not altogether sober passenger's reflections on his fellow passengers' existential sphere of concern, assigning a subordinate position to the belongings mentioned on the loudspeakers while a reflecting and caring we is introduced?

In a flash, the notion of reality is being turned upside down and you recoil, with surprise.

Unexpectedly, the predictability of the situation is being replaced by something meaningful on a level lying beyond the implications of the factual statements. Between two moments of awareness – in a crack in time – a shift in the level of consciousness occurs and separates two essentially different modes of reasoning and contents of consciousness.

This imperceptible wordless crack in time is the very now– the Golden Moment – enriched by an insight lying beyond the here and now. Feeling uplifted and strangely lighthearted, I continued on my way through central Copenhagen – having been reminded once again that something precious about humanity is worth keeping an eye on and that areas that are of concern to me are significant to others as well.

This insightful space is so essentially different from the moment of receiving an apparently factual piece of information which, in a flash, separates us from our confidence in the basic goodness of humanity. This is similar to experiencing – in a jarring moment's loss of identity –

that somebody has stolen our wallet, with its various credit- and identity-cards, at a railway station.

Interpretations of reality

It is obvious that the announcement from the loudspeakers indicates that an increasing number of thefts are occurring at railway stations and public spaces. From what we are reading in the newspapers and hearing from other news outlets, it is well-known that the open borders within the EU have resulted in the influx, into the countries of Western Europe, of a growing number of Eastern Europeans, who do not have the same access to material wealth as we have: people who allegedly are well-versed in rather sophisticated ways of misappropriating valuables from us unsuspecting and trusting Danes.

So when the announcement from the train's loudspeakers plays, we know precisely what is being said as well as what lies implicitly behind the words. Depending on the disposition, attitude and interpretation of the passengers – who have not yet become immune to the message as a consequence of its constant repetition – the message's declamation may give rise to a wealth of fantasies and interpretations of reality that revolve around this theme: spreading out in the immediate vicinity are Eastern Europeans who've got one thing in mind, namely to steal your wallet, your credit card, your mobile phone, your computer, or any other valuables you might have in your possession.

Little by little, we get used to accepting and integrating this perception of reality as a mental formation of our consciousness. In addition, we are busy preparing the ground for incorporating and legitimizing a generalized perception of the situation and its potential hazards that also covers other areas of the public domain. A mental and emotional state of alert, with which we meet reality, is assumed – and for safety's sake, we take our precautions.

We gradually get used to perceiving and handling reality from the vantage point of this conception: having acquired material amenities, some of which we carry around and perceive as our natural equipment – the way the world is today – we have to be careful not to be robbed by people who also want and need these things but who apparently cannot acquire them legally.

The way we think about and approach reality gradually becomes integrated in our habitual mental pattern so that we automatically act appropriately in any given situation. With this, everything is in control, at least until new ways of being robbed are developed, for instance, in our homes or on the Internet. But that can also be managed, in that a new industry will promptly emerge, as a reaction to this, to safeguard our belongings – for a fee.

Selective Distrust
We learn to be on our guard, which may be quite reasonable. But the day we walk down the street and discover that we are not safe around people who look different or who clearly do not appear to be average, reasonably well-off people, we are being confronted by an interpretation of reality that indicates that we have more or less consciously incorporated a view of humanity and reality that is based on selective distrust.

It is tempting to speak of a kind of "everyday paranoia" which elucidates that we are dealing with a fear-based albeit an altogether normal, mundane, and harmless distortion of our perception of reality. But this distortion manifests itself as an interpretation of reality that goes far beyond the fact that it might be perfectly relevant to be extra vigilant in certain situations where pickpocketing might conceivably occur.

The pattern of thought, which is related from the outset to a specific situation with one possible course of development, come to be expanded, through generalizations, to cover an increasing field of places and situations where the event *might* occur – you begin to see it happening everywhere. At the same time, a generalization about the – otherwise purely imaginary – strange, foreign, destitute and thieving person sets in. Thus, conceptions about a growing but nonetheless limited group of people are being formed in our consciousness, characterizing those people as being different and therefore strange, a group of people whom we perceive as being destitute and therefore in quest of our valuables.

This fear-based interpretation of reality generates a more and more entrenched and partly instinctual thought pattern that imperceptibly tends to become self-reinforcing. It contributes to bringing about a form of tunnel vision that precludes other points of view and perceptions of reality and other approaches to being in the world.

Such fixed thought patterns, when they are fully unfolded, may appear real to us. We experience them not merely as true depictions of reality but as reality itself. However, if we give ourselves the time to reflect on the situation and to survey it a little bit from above, we might come to realize, that we – perhaps contrary to our self-perception and our outlook on life – are harboring prejudices. Prejudices that are supported by – and that are legitimizing – a certain interpretation of reality. An ostensibly necessary "attitude of crisis management" and an appurtenant "coping strategy" are more or less consciously activated in order to keep fear at bay. And we regain the feeling of being in control and empowered.

The legitimization of selective distrust appears to gain official sanction by virtue of being broadcast in the public space of communication by the authorities that are responsible for public transport, regardless of whether this is the intention or not. It might thus facilitate an interpretation of the message that validates our fear and distrust toward a certain group of fellow human beings in society – without even having to think very closely about this.

Fixed mental structures and neural networks

Thought structures that are not subjected to reflection and reconsideration will become fixed and will result in the constriction of not only our thinking and our field of consciousness but also of our brain functions. Fixed thought structures can remain unchallenged as an upshot of mental laziness. Or we might feel that we have too much to take into consideration and when we are consequently confronted with a growing sense of impotence, we opt for the easy solution of floating along unreflectively with the news flow and the common understanding. The ongoing development of fixations of thought structures thus tends to be underpinned by collectively established views and outlooks on life.

In extraordinary cases – for instance, with fanatics and fundamentalists, as well as in cases of personality disorders – a permanently fixed mental and emotional fear-based structure can crystallize in the mind. This might eventually block the person's natural ability to think rationally and reasonably and to be empathic and compassionate.

Recent cognitive and neuroscience research supports the supposition that the formation of mental structures and the formation of neural networks run parallel to each other. The neural networks can, in the manner of mental structures, form fixed patterns that are automatically activated in certain situations, resulting in the suppression of activity in other parts of the brain. This is seen, for instance, when a person experiences being in a hazardous situation over an extended time. In such cases, brain activity will be centered in the part of the brain that deals with fighting or fleeing the danger. The higher brain functions that are active when we think, analyze, reflect and solve problems, and when we are being empathic and compassionate will then, to a greater or lesser extent, be dominated by areas of the brain that support an automatic impulse behavior driven by instincts related to survival. These neural networks, having been built up over time, may come to dominate the workings of the brain and eventually limit its capacity and range.

If, however, something unexpected occurs, we may be pushed out of our rigid perception-structure. Like when, in a flash, the apparently not perfectly sober passenger's reflection, with a single stroke, caused the words and the concept to enter into a new realm of meaning.

At the very basic level, most people know that our tendency to render ourselves unaware of our own thought patterns, for example, by forming prejudices, serves as a filter for experiencing the world around us: a covering-up of our sense of resignation and impotence when we happen to be confronted with a reality that feels increasingly overwhelming, complex, and at times threatening. Especially because we increasingly feel empty-handed and incapable of catching sight of anything in ourselves with which we could face the ever-changing challenges of the times.

This self-protective mechanism for rendering ourselves unaware and for shielding ourselves from seeing reality and ourselves in all the aspects of life and existence is perhaps the most inadequate safety precaution we could grasp for, because:

- **Unawareness not only shields us from being confronted with aspects of reality that seem overwhelming and unbearable.**

- **Unawareness also separates us from resources that are necessary for coping with the conditions – i.e. rational thinking, reflection, and empathy.**

- **Unawareness prevents us from realizing and taking to heart that every one of us is a co-creator of the circumstances that form our individual and our collective reality.**

Reflection and investigation

Our experience bears out that it is often in situations in which we feel hurt and vulnerable that we are most motivated to be open and to listen to a "deeper" intelligence within ourselves: an intelligence and a sense of knowing that may change our perception so that we see the situation in a completely new perspective.

"When God closes a door, He opens a window" is a figure of speech we employ when entirely new possibilities suddenly appear at a moment when we feel most powerless and derailed. When what we wanted, hoped for, and expected simply did not transpire or when we were bowled over by events that crucially changed the conditions of our life. Behind this figure of speech lies our utterly unique ability to learn, to reflect and to change perspective when something goes terribly awry or when something happens in ways that we did not expect it to happen. The experience of becoming wiser can be so uplifting that what went wrong no longer has power over us and it loses its significance. This new appreciation of the situation becomes a turning point and we experience unexpected openings and we find ourselves already moving ahead on a new track.

This ability to transform a hopeless situation by reflecting, investigating and rethinking and by spotting entirely new possibilities characterizes us as human beings in everyday occurrences as well as when we are facing radical changes. This ability to change perspective and act accordingly is probably a contributory factor in our survival as a species on Earth.

Perhaps we are standing right now at a juncture in human history in which we need to remind ourselves, more than ever before, that we do have this ability – individually, as well as on the societal level, and perhaps, for the first time in history, on a global level.

In the field of crisis psychology, it is well-known that in order to cope with a traumatizing situation and subsequently heal the trauma, a person needs to be in contact with his or her own resources and qualities – resources and qualities that he or she is reminded of in the course of the therapeutic treatment of the trauma – and that have presumably been untouched by the trauma. Thus, in a trauma-therapy session, the person is supported in regaining contact with potentials that enable him or her to gradually confront and heal the traumatic situation. [25]

We can find something similar in the personal accounts of people who, for instance, during wars and in concentration camps, have experienced inhumane treatment, the violation of basic human values and threats posed to their lives. Evidently, those who – in spite of unspeakable humiliation and constant danger to their lives – managed to maintain and deepen their contact with profoundly human values were the ones that stood the greatest chance of surviving. One outstanding example is the Austrian neurologist and psychiatrist, Victor Frankl, a Holocaust survivor

---

[25] Levine, 2004

who subsequently managed to create a deeply meaningful life for himself and was able to help others, as well. [26]

Another testimony to this that stems from our own time can be found in Ingrid Betancourt's autobiographical book, *Even Silence Has an End: My Six Years of Captivity in the Colombian Jungle*. Her book is an account of the time she spent as a hostage in the hands of the FARC guerillas. [27] During her captivity, while she was chained, starved and subjected to humiliating abuse and constant death threats, she realized that the most important freedom, which no one could take away from her, was *the freedom to choose what kind of person she wanted to be*. It was this realization that made her understand that she was no longer a victim: she was free to choose to hate or not. She was a survivor. This realization was the beginning of an inner exploration, where Betancourt chose to insist on maintaining her dignity as a human being. She makes no secret of her own selfish propensities and tendencies toward pettiness but observes and reports everything with harrowing honesty. Because she understood that thinking and acting out of pure motives nurtured everything meaningful and valuable in life. The experience of inner strength and personal integrity was inextricably linked to the victories she eventually won, both by conquering her own inner weaknesses and by being able to withstand the brutality and the humiliations suffered in the prison camp. Being completely human, she adamantly refused to identify with the powerlessness that characterizes the inhumane relation between victim and torturer.

Is humanity losing its influence?

The reality that we, as mankind, find ourselves in at the beginning of the 21st century does not seem to be playing itself out as expected. One of the upshots of this is, to a certain extent, our becoming accustomed to not expecting anything – just to be on the safe side.

The experience of having lost influence, both individually and collectively, can be traced in a loss of confidence that we are actually able to leave any mark on our reality and regard ourselves as co-creators of our futures. Personal and collective efforts no longer seem to have the same significance that would bear on the outcome of events. We cannot be sure that our endeavors are going to bear the fruits we envisioned and that were foreseen. This is, in itself, a gravely serious state of affairs. However, we need to realize that we are not dealing only with a lack of predictability, broken promises and disappointments. It appears that **something has gone utterly wrong.**

---

26 Frankl, 2004
27 Betancourt, 2010

We are increasingly witnessing that the measures taken to bring societies and individuals back to "the right course" in wake of the global financial crises in 2008 are not quite yielding the desired results and that reforms that have been provoked by the crisis seem, in many instances, to be worsening the situation for more and more people. Young people who went along with predictions for what society would need from them in terms of education cannot get employment after having finished their education. Many employees in their future fields have, in the meantime, been fired due to cutbacks – and many jobs have disappeared.

The medical sociologist Aaron Antonovsky who, in a scientific study, analyzed matters of fundamental importance to the physical and mental health of humans, coined the notion: "Sense of Coherence" (SOC). [28] The parameters that Antonovsky found to be crucial to our health were related to the fulfillment of three expectations: 1) that we believe new situations are susceptible to our efforts; 2) that the situation we are in is logical and predictable; and 3) that what is demanded of us in new situations is manageable. Thus, according to Antonovsky, what is fundamental to good physical and mental health is that we are able to participate and that we are capable of achieving what we set out to achieve when we are confronted with new situations, and that we experience the situations as being coherent and promising. It is also important that the demands posed by the situation do not decisively exceed our capabilities.

A sense of unpredictability and incapacitation along with the feeling of having our abilities over-extended is a growing experience amongst the general public. This poses a serious threat to our health. The question is, how did it get this far.

Reality deprivation

We have apparently been carried forth on a wave of incessant progress, economic growth and change. In the more prosperous parts of the world, citizens have access to extensive opportunities for mobility, exchange and expression. The momentous changes have occurred on a scale and at a rate that are unparalleled in the history of mankind. This has contributed to bringing about a change in our perception of time and our collective perception of ourselves as human beings and of life on the whole. This we find mirrored, for example, in a change of language usage.

The phrase "a child of its time" expresses that we hold common human traits with which we identify ourselves, individually and collectively,

---

28 Antonovsky, 1979

and that we are also marked by the culture and the social conditions at any given point in time. During the 20th century, as industrialization influenced more and more areas of life, the phrase "a product of his or her time" was coined. The rate of change that we are experiencing today renders both expressions obsolete. There is, so to speak, no time to be a "child of our time" and the built-in outmodedness of products becomes effective in the very moment such products are put into circulation as commodities. A more precise characterization would seem to be: "capitalizing humanity for future material growth". [29]

The question many people are asking themselves is: *what future*? And why are our expectations of and our ideas about the future – whether they harbor fear or hope – so important that we literally live for the future at the expense of the present, without really being in touch with what we can actually accomplish right now?

The dominant growth paradigm, which has been focused on the measurable and quantitative assessment of product outcome, increasingly perceives and assesses human beings according to their efficiency when it comes to manufacturing products and obtaining results. Even in the fields of social services, healthcare, education and science, the dominant focus is currently on the results obtained by quantifying care, teaching, learning, and the outcome of research, respectively. We are expected to meet future "deadlines" and to fulfill contracts with a certain future outcome in mind. How we are presently carrying out our professional and personal skills and individual qualities appears to be of secondary importance.

The predominantly linear perception of time that unfurls itself across the time-axis, running from the past, via the present, to the future, tends, in many ways, to de-emphasize the notion of space of time, in which events occur simultaneously. This runs the risk of depriving humanity of a pivotal dimension of existence. And accordingly, dwelling in "the now" has increasingly become unfamiliar to us. While focusing on the forward-looking time axis and on the results to be achieved, the impression gleaned is that we are being forced to hurry along. Apparently, we are thus being subjected to a collective elimination of the present.

The dilemma, then, is: how can we possibly point out a development and a forward-looking perspective of the future when reading the present with awareness, insight and presence is hardly topical? When we actually do take the present seriously, it is primarily by means of quan-

---
[29] Praetorius, 2002

tifying what is taking place. An example can be seen in the so-called "quality management", which is articulated in measures like standardized functional descriptions and the time-allocation of work and learning, as well as in evaluation schemes that quantitatively gauge the resulting achievements.

> *The precedence of the linear and one-dimensional time axis over the experience of the "space of time" and simultaneity conceptions as well as the tendency to deal mainly with quantity-related measurement at the expense of examining quality constitute a considerable limitation of humanity's field of reality. This entails, in reality, a devaluing of humanity and a reduction in our possibilities of self-perception and self-expression.*

This deprivation of reality not only affects our existential sense of belonging in life but also affects our being in and our handling of the present. As will be clarified in Chapter 5, this also has repercussions on the natural process of maturing as a human being. Engaging in an attentive presence of the now, in mutual exchange with others, constitutes a precondition for getting to know oneself and the world. This, on its part, is the precondition for developing our potentials and qualities optimally.

The human involvement

Becoming emancipated from the disempowering experience of having been robbed of personal influence presupposes a fundamental shift in perspective regarding ourselves and the situation in which we are standing. At a time when the mindset and the approaches of the neoliberal market society no longer appear to be in keeping with the times – and can even be said, at that, to be counterproductive – it seems crucial that we muster the courage to reinstate ourselves as co-creators of reality. From this point of departure, we are able to form completely new visions for humanity and for the world. This may have a high-falutin', idealistic ring to it. But what is the alternative?

For many years, the overall responsibility for the shape and the management of our democratic society has been left in the hands of a sphere of elected officials and administrators – a cadre that is increasingly influenced by powerful financial institutions and their interests. It would seem to be increasingly urgent that the individual's sense of responsibility, active involvement, knowledge and competences be valued and incorporated to a far greater extent, on all levels of society.

As has been mentioned in Chapter 1, a growing number of economists, social theorists and scientists who are dealing with the development of sustainable technology and who are involved in the study of new opportunities brought about by globalization are advocating the development of a new political and ethical philosophy for the Global Age – an ethical way of thinking that takes our mutual dependency across cultures and borders into account and, along with this, the necessity to cooperate in solving the challenges of our day. Time and time again, what is stressed is that human involvement based on knowledge and the wish to make an effort for the common good are preconditions for creating changes based on humanitarian values and democratic principles. [30] [31]

The previous centuries brought forth a number of people who proposed necessary changes in the prevailing mindset and in the makeup of society. These individuals and their followers advocated initially for fairer and more humanitarian conditions for the citizens. Regardless of how appealing these ideas might have seemed, originally, unfolding these proposed measures in the real world as they were envisioned has proven to be very difficult. Perhaps this is not due so much to the conceptual framework of the measures proposed but rather to what is typically a restricted effort that was made to seriously integrate the recommended ideas and values – not sometime off in the distant future when a better society would hopefully have become a reality - but rather as a parallel measure in the realization of the desired social conditions.

Proponents of new social values and societal makeups are themselves, for better or worse, examples of the ideas and values they embody. With a few poignant exceptions in our own time, for instance, Mahatma Gandhi, Martin Luther King and Nelson Mandela, it is evident that leaders and initiators of innovative movements have only to a limited extent stood as living examples of their declared values and views of humanity.

Ideologically-based social theories that have played a dominant role since the late 19th century are built on the assumption that management rationales and societal institutions, in accordance with a given ideological conception of society, have to be established first. Only subsequent to this has an overall adjustment of attitude, behavior and thinking – aimed toward adapting people to the intended make-up of society – been considered timely.

---

30 Held, 2010
31 Jackson, 2009

The German social scientist Jürgen Habermas has challenged this view on matters. In his re-framing of critical theory, he emphasizes the significance of emancipation. Criticizing Marx, Habermas points out that the reduction and reification of humanity occurs when human beings are subjected to and perceived as being determined primarily by political economy and social conditions. [32]

Also the German social psychologist Harald Welzer has dealt extensively with the transformation of "mental infrastructure" i.e. a way of thinking and self-perception that has resulted from current socioeconomic changes and the demands for the attitude- and behavior-adjustment of citizens in order to achieve the requirements posed by neoliberal growth societies. [33]

A reductionist and dehumanized perception of humanity is practiced not only by authoritarian and dictatorial, "socialist" and fascist regimes. With the introduction of neoliberalism into the Western democratic societies, at the end of the 20th century we have witnessed the very same practice. This and the consequences hereof will be dealt with in the following chapters.

Notwithstanding the sociopolitical changes taking their point of departure in ideologically-based theory which have been attempted, we have unfortunately played witness to a corruption of not just the ideas but of the people, too – a corruption that often sets in, at first, on the level of leadership and management. This has occurred when the struggle for power, prestige and economic means – a struggle that is going on both internally and externally – has invariably undermined the realization of the original ideas. This provides the grounds for emphasizing that a new world order and social structure need to be founded not only on the formulation of new global policy and a new ethical philosophy. Equally crucial is a progressive maturing of ethical attitudes and of the ethical behavior of individuals, be they leaders or be they ordinary citizen. [34]

Existential choices

If we wish to make existential choices that affect ourselves and the world, it is necessary – although not sufficient – that we be familiar with the external life circumstances in which we find ourselves, as well as with the changes we find to be necessary.

---

32 Habermas, 1968
33 Welzer, 2011
34) Rifkin, 2010

Furthermore, we need to be fully aware of how we are equipped, of how we best function and how we best develop as human beings. We need to be fully aware of what makes us thrive, and why. If we do not take the trouble to gain insight into, and to acquire personal knowledge about, something that is altogether fundamental about being human, our attempts to create new circumstances of life will run the risk of resting on abstract assumptions, habitual notions and pious hopes. In other words, ideal notions that may turn out, after all is said and done, to being nothing other than repetitions that are clad in a new disguise of unreflective assumptions about what it is to be human and about what characterizes human communities. This would be something like attempting to build a new house on worn-out foundations.

In the following section, we will be taking a closer look at various categories of theories about humanity and at their underlying assumptions and views about the fundamental nature of mankind.

The theories constitute some portion of the handed-down ways of thinking that we, to a greater or lesser extent, have been taking for granted and have identified ourselves with.

The purpose of starting off with a short account of the aforementioned theories and of their view of humanity and human societies is to offer an idea of the way they affect our perception, our notion of ourselves, and our way of life. The purpose of this exposition is to create space for reflection and possibly reconsideration. The theories about humanity and society that are going to be presented and examined here, and in the following chapters, will therefore be considered and scrutinized in order to elucidate whether and how they might potentially be helpful and whether and how they might otherwise set up obstacles to the self-determination of humanity.

Theories about humanity

Theories about humanity and the scientific methods take their point of departure in basic assumptions or stipulations about certain fundamental aspects of being human, regardless of whether these are stated explicitly or not. [35] The prevalent theories can roughly be divided into the three following categories:

---

35) Israel, 1972. Joachim Israel distinguishes between three types of statements: value statements; descriptive statements; and stipulations. Like value statements, stipulations are normative in character, insofar as they concern the nature of humanity and society and are incorporated as pivotal, often tacit preconditions in psychological and social-scientific theories

1. 1. Theories that subscribe to a view of humanity springing from the assumption that human biological and genetic make-up and functioning are fundamental to the way we behave and develop. From the viewpoint of this perspective, we are predominantly controlled by impulses, instincts and drives that are seated in the brain. These predispositions operate in cooperation with the brain to facilitate the self-expression that is required for the individual and the species to survive. In this category, we find philosophical, medical and psychological lines of thought that ascribe pivotal importance to our genetic and biological make-up and to the brain's functions. [36]

2. 2. Theories that explicitly take their point of departure in the assumption that certain basic preconditions characterize humanity and distinguish human beings from other creatures. These are potentials, abilities and qualities that are regarded as being innately human. Psychological and philosophical currents concerned with basic human functions like thinking, feeling and conscious awareness would belong to this category of theories about humanity.

3. 3. Theories in this category refrain from dealing with basic human preconditions and the biological make-up and functioning of the human brain. These theories may, for instance, adhere to the notion that human beings are constructs formed in relation to their socio-cultural conditions. In this theoretical framework, language and linguistic rules are basic to – and constitute – human beings. Social-constructivist and systemic theories can be seen as examples of this category of theories about humanity. [37]

The theories about the nature of human beings within the different schools of thought provide very different perceptions and knowledge about us and our being in the world. Fundamental disparities between the pre-scientific assumptions or stipulations might thus lead to mutually contradictory views, descriptions and theories about being human.

Quantitative research methodologies

Research within biology and neuroscience and within social-constructivism will primarily make use of so-called objective, quantitative meth-

---

[36] Houshmand et al., 1999. Physicalism within, e.g., neuroscience is manifested in the assumption that mental states spring from the physical brain which, in other words, is producing mind.

[37]) As will be outlined in the following chapter, relational theories may – regardless of the fact that they operate with subject and object, with an I and a Thou – nonetheless consider this I and Thou abstractly, which contributes to the very reification being explicitly repudiated.

odologies, whereby behavior becomes the object of observation and recording. The very objects of the research – human beings and the relationships between them – are observed from the outside by the researcher. The object of research is kept within and determined by clearly demarcated functions and areas.

This, however, does not preclude the gathering of verbal statements about mental and emotional experiences and sensations, which are duly processed and interpreted and subsequently incorporated as research results. Subjective statements will typically be collected as quantifiable data, attained through various structured data-collection techniques. Among these are, for example, interviews or questionnaires in which the subject's reports and responses are specified and delimited by statements that have been worded by the researcher. The subject evaluates these statements – for instance, by making multiple-choice or graded numerical scale assessments. Furthermore, statistical accounts will typically be used to render probable and offer evidence of causal connections as well as evidence of the effects of interplay among various factors that are the object of the research activity. By way of example, one could mention effect studies that are being conducted within the pharmaceutical industry. These research methodologies have been transferred to social science disciplines like sociology and psychology.

Qualitative research methodologies

Within the existential field of research – belonging to the above mentioned category 2 - primarily qualitative research methodology is applied. The subjects' experiences obtained, for instance, through introspective and phenomenological methods are included as research data. Research data obtained through introspection based on the subjects' own statements and personal experiences, reflections and insights are thus considered legitimate approaches to obtaining reliable and valid research data.

Phenomenology is the study of how the world and its phenomena present themselves to us. The phenomenological method is central in research that seeks to explore and understand qualitative aspects of human beings and our experience of ourselves and the world. Within contemporary philosophy, phenomenology is generally understood as being a research method, the aim of which is the study of human experience. Phenomenological, introspective analysis attempts to move beyond preconceived ideas and habitual perceptions and to approach experiencing events and phenomena open-mindedly, as they present themselves for the person. For Edmund Husserl, the founder of modern phenomenology, the first-person perspective and the human consciousness are core concepts. [38]

Phenomenology is critical of empiricism and positivism, which deal exclusively with what can be observed objectively, or from the outside, and supposedly without any prior assumptions being made about the observed. This latter scientific perspective has, however, set the pace and has become norm-giving for the last 60-70 years in the research of psychology and sociology to an extent that qualitative approaches have apparently been left without scientific legitimacy and consequently left in the lurch without much economic funding. [39]

Methodological considerations

So-called "evidence-based research", which supposedly generates objectively true research results, presently appears to have been elevated up to a scientific ideal. It is, of course, prudent and relevant to speak of evidence-based research results when the research deals with very simple causal relations: for instance, when we want to demonstrate the effect of a certain drug on certain diseases. However, this method is hardly suitable for dealing with more complex matters, like when we are dealing with highly varied and changeable causal relations that pertain to human well being or the lack thereof, as well as to attitudes, behavior and mental states. Furthermore, new perspectives might prove, within the compass of a short time, to be more relevant, thus nullifying the current "evidence-based" results.

Contrasting this approach is hermeneutics, which was developed as a philosophical school of thought in the 20th century by, among others, the German philosopher Hans-Georg Gadamer. The point of departure here is an assumption that human beings understand the world by experiencing and interpreting it. [40] For the hermeneutic thinkers and the phenomenologists, it makes no sense to speak of objectivity in an absolute sense. Research that is based on so-called objective, quantitative methods can thus, from this perspective of understanding, not claim any monopoly on reliability and validity in favor of research that is based on subjective and qualitative methods.

---

38 Welton, 1999
39 Phenomenology has gained ground within sociology, represented by Pierre Bourdieu and Anthony Giddens; within Gestalt psychology, represented by Kurt Koffka, Wolfgang Köhler and Edgar Rubin; as well as within humanistic psychology, represented by Abraham Maslow and Rollo May
40 Gadamer, 2004

Thus, hermeneutics offers a critique of scientific approaches that lay claim to being objective: interpretation is undeniably taking place although this is patently denied. The central fulcrum of the critique is that remaining aware that we are not dealing with objective, universal, and absolute knowledge is more appropriate than succumbing to the delusion that there is such a thing as objective, true knowledge.

A similar line of argument can be found when we move from the humanities over into contemporary scientific paradigms within the field of physics, and specifically into Niels Bohr's philosophical and meta-theoretical considerations related to the development of quantum physics. According to Bohr, the purpose of experimental observations and measurements is not to describe – in an absolute sense – an objective reality but rather to examine a "communicable human experience" about observed reality. This position springs from a realization that what is being observed will always be subordinate to the method of observation. Understanding and knowledge acquired through the research process is necessarily determined by both the scientist's previous knowledge and understanding and by the method being utilized. Furthermore, Bohr states, that the very research process influences the object of exploration. [41]

The uncertainty principle of quantum physics – which states that it impossible to precisely measure both the position and the speed of a subatomic particle simultaneously – as well as the controversial philosophical statement that the world is only perceivable when it is measured and thus not perceivable as nature in itself – has spawned a great deal of discussion and uncertainty about the field of validity subsumed by the theories that we put forward about the phenomena of reality. The inevitability of this uncertainty was even supported by Bohr when he expressed the basic observation that we cannot separate the behavior of atomic entities from their interaction with the measuring instrument, which unavoidably delimits and determines the conditions under which the phenomena elapse. [42]

Albert Einstein's statement that physical concepts are the free inventions of human beings and that they cannot be said to be determined by an outer world further emphasizes that knowledge achieved through science is conditioned by concepts and viewpoints that we apply to what we want to explore. [43]

---
41 Richard & Thuan, 2001
42 Bohr, 1958
43 Einstein & Infeld, 1938

The advances of modern mathematics and physics – and along with these, the explosive technological developments – have supplied altogether robust evidence for their considerable fields of validity in practice. At the same time, the demonstration of the essential limitations of classical rational thought has influenced other scientific areas, for instance, critical philosophy and social science. Thus so-called "value-free research" has been called into question and the normative reality creation of research has been put up for discussion. [44]

It is remarkable that there is still no prevailing consensus within the human sciences about the idea that theories and descriptions of humanity and reality are basically mediations of reality viewed through specific systems of concepts and meaning at a given time. Theories and research results, accordingly, cannot lay claim to being objective and ultimately true representations of reality. However, any interest in new scientific paradigms and meta-theoretical considerations appears to be rather limited within research areas like medicine, psychology and the social sciences

Rational bypassing and Complementarity

The precedence of rational thought over the introspective approach to developing knowledge originated – as was pointed out in Chapter 1 – in the wake of Enlightenment, during the advent of rationalism, some 400 years ago. Subjective and qualitative observation associated with metaphysical and religious conceptions, assumptions and dogmas, in the grip of which humanity had been held for centuries, eventually lost its methodological legitimacy. In its stead, objective and predominantly quantitative ways of exploring, recording, and obtaining information about reality were considered to be the correct methodology. Thus, what I call "rational bypassing" was institutionalized as scientific practice.

These two approaches, however, may very well complement each other. Whereas qualitative methods get to the core of the matter and strive to unravel and understand the nature, the being, and the function of the object under examination, quantitative methods can demonstrate causal relations on both the micro and macro levels. Thus, there need not necessarily be any inherent incongruity between describing and understanding phenomena and their being-in-the-world and the demonstration of observable relations and mutual exchanges between phenomena. In the same way, rational thought and logical inference are not necessarily incompatible with gaining insight through introspection. On the contrary, these two ways of gaining knowledge can be seen as being

---
44 Israel, J., 1972; Israel, S.B., 2011

mutually invigorating and productive. Furthermore, a healing of the artificial schism in the capacity of the human mind could serve to facilitate the deployment of a wide range of subjective categories of experience, whereby we are capable of perceiving and experiencing mind and reality multi-dimensionally.

A complementarity perspective would allow us to experience and realize that there is no reason to entrench oneself in an either-or mindset of giving quantitative statements precedence over qualitative statements. Likewise, "time-axis time" and "time as space of time" could be appreciated as equally relevant ways of approaching time and being in time.

In the following chapters the absence of an attitude of complementary will be shown to have repercussions for the application of technology and for the lack of ethical considerations and hence its damaging effects.

Humanity in an all-embracing perspective

Research that is striving to see and understand man from an all-embracing perspective incorporates methods and knowledge from all three of the categories of theories about humanity outlined above. The latest scientific research thus seems to show that the biological make-up of human beings and the function of the brain and the development and maturation of the basic capacities constituting human beings are related in mutual interdependency. The same can be said when it comes to the historical, physical and socio-cultural context in which human beings exist and evolve.

When an all-embracing perspective is recommended in this book, this springs from a realization that there is no particular one of the aforementioned categories of theory which, by itself, is sufficient for dealing with the progressive acquisition of knowledge about the development of man's physical, mental and emotional capacity and potential. Such an all-embracing view is pivotal to shedding light on both the opportunities we have as well as on the obstacles that confront us, individually and collectively, in our attempts to face the challenge that constitutes the overall concern of the book. Ergo, it seems of vital importance that we be open to a varied and multidimensional approach if we really want to develop a new paradigm and develop new ways of living as human beings.

The complex human being

The relation of mutual interdependency that can be observed between different levels of activity and functions in human beings does not imply that we are always dealing with relations of functioning "intelligently" and with relations that have a unifying, constructive and balancing effect on each other. Human beings – especially when we move beyond the biological level – cannot be described as predictable systems that are intrinsically striving toward a beneficial functionality and equilibrium of the system.

On the contrary, in the study of human functioning and self-expression, we are constantly confronted with apparently paradoxical and contradictory phenomena that bear witness to the fact that we, as human beings, are rather complex. Our thoughts, opinions and feelings, and our actions toward ourselves, toward others, and toward the surrounding environment appear from time to time to be downright unpredictable, erratic and impractical.

More or less consciously, we can be consumed by self-interest and occupied with obtaining whatever satisfies our needs – i.e. with the fulfillment of biological drives and desires or with the attainment of basic necessities. Or we find ourselves to be indulging, to varying degrees, in the search for a lucrative position, for prestige, for power and for economic advantages. In such situations, we act as if we were being compelled to do so by some insensitive and mindless force, aimed at attaining, by any means necessary, whatever will lead to satisfaction and aimed at repelling whatever might be standing in our way – and with little concern for others.

In other situations, we may find ourselves thinking, behaving and acting selflessly, with the intention of benefitting others, regardless of whatever sacrifice this entails for us.

There will also be times when we reflect upon this apparent paradox and wish that we, once in a while, were capable of restraining ourselves and being less egoistic, self-centered and inconsiderate toward others. Upon reflection, we may come to feel really badly when others approach us inattentively, and often, when we come to grips with a sense of our own thoughtlessness, we regret this kind of behavior and attitude. Such reflections are the precondition for our consciously choosing to shape **our thoughts and behavior in a more humane direction in the course of maturing as human beings.**

That we are subject to both our biology and to our worldview and the reigning norms in our socio-cultural context does not entail that the way we are in the world is conditioned unambiguously by these. Our human makeup – as has been suggested – is also characterized by the possibility and the freedom to be reflective and consciously choose to rise above and emancipate ourselves from the constraints of both instinctual biological behavioral patterns and socially and culturally determined concepts about reality.

The rediscovery of direct experience
The existential point of departure that is being advanced in this book presents a frame of understanding that builds on pre-theoretical assumptions about uniquely human qualities and potentials. Among these is our potential of transcending and liberating ourselves from both outer and inner conditioning. The basic inherent capacity of human beings to be empathic, compassionate, altruistic and self-forgetting, is regarded as a fundamental potential that we can chose to consciously ripen and unfold as part of our coming-into-being in our lives. Thus, our capacity to directly experiencing ourselves and the surrounding world and our potential to appreciate and realize countless ways of exchanging the necessities of life among the inhabitants of Earth is right at hand. This is going to be indispensable when it comes to realizing new departures related to being in the world.

Furthermore, it's up to every one of us to learn in the direct experience in the cracks in time – in a split second's glimpse of insight, creativity and emphatic presence – that we are left with an indisputable certainty: a certainty that stems from having experienced that reality, playing itself out in infinite manifestations of thoughts, actions and life, is a variation on something wordless and original. Something directly accessible and intact within us that confirms that we are so much more than the apparently endless abstractions, notions and theories that we concoct about existence and about ourselves.

Perhaps we will come to realize that the conditioned perception of reality and the experience of inner alienation, which inevitably supervenes as a consequence of the separation from the direct experience of altogether original human potentials and qualities, do not represent a view of reality the we have to content ourselves with at all times. No more than we need to let ourselves be controlled by instinct- and fear-based, irrational interpretations of reality that tend to reinforce the separation from our human foundation – the very foundation of something that is basically healthy and true within us.

The gracious space of compassion

In a wondrous way, reality caught up with me while I was busy writing this chapter. Completely unexpected and unannounced, I met an Eastern European man a short while ago. I did not meet an abstraction in the shape of a preconceived attitude like the one I could easily have formed when I heard a warning that we had to keep an eye on our belongings being spoken from the loudspeakers on the commuter train. No, this was a young Romanian, in the flesh, whom I encountered on the sidewalk outside the emergency room at a hospital in Copenhagen.

The encounter became one of the Golden Moments that occur when we – regardless of the conditioning we experience from our own times, from social constructions, from the function of the brain, and from habitual mental structures – encounter ourselves and the other at a depth of humanity in which just that is present. It was this young Romanian man – ragged, grimy, and starving – who opened up that space for both of us and then took his leave from there when we parted. For this, I am deeply grateful and indebted to him.

> *I was standing, feeling insecure and disoriented, and was holding myself propped up with the aid of a pair of crutches that I had received, along with a boot-like splint, at the emergency room. An unending course of examinations and waiting around came to its conclusion with finding that I had contracted a nasty sprain and a fracture in my foot, following my having suffered an unlucky fall on the stairs. Exerting what seemed, after the hours spent at the emergency room, to be the very last of my strength, I managed to drag myself outside and was now waiting – on this late-summer Sunday night, in the dusk – to be picked up by a good friend.*

> The automatic door-opener of the emergency room sounded behind me and when I turned around, a young man came staggering, with shaky steps, toward me. Hunched over, and with flailing arms that were gesticulating into the air, he cried out, in agony, almost proclaiming: "I am already dead, I am already dead." After a short pause, he continued: "I want to kill, I want to kill. It does not matter, I am already dead. I am so hungry, SO HUNGRY". And he hunched over, even further forward, as if he wanted to relieve the pain in that hollow space of his stomach. "I will kill, and go to jail for the rest of my life, and I will get food every day. I will stay in jail always and get food."

> As if he had only now spotted me, he made a pause in his repeated, sustained and desperate cries. Then he continued, insistently, and

aimed his utterance directly at me: "Tell me that you understand me. Tell me that you understand me!"

We were completely alone outside the emergency room and after a split second's realization that I was standing entirely exposed to the situation, in my own way, as was he, for his part, I answered him, with all the weight my sincerity could give the words: "I do understand you. I do understand you!"

For a while, he continued vividly describing his plight and his wish to kill ... and urged me intermittently to answer that I understood him. That, I did.

As he eventually calmed down, he began speaking about the horrifying conditions in Romania, where a small percent of the population has acquired immense wealth for themselves and where young people without any means of feeding themselves are completely at the mercy of the mafia and the gangs and he declared that he would be a dead man the day he returned to Romania.

I conceded that this was terrible and that changing the conditions would be necessary. I said that we have to have confidence that it is possible.

Mid-conversation, a nurse came out from the emergency room bearing a form that they had forgotten to give me. At first, she scrutinized me and then she scrutinized the young man, whereupon she hastily returned inside again.

As he returned to the thought of doing something desperate, I earnestly urged him to seek out a shelter where he would be fed and given a bed in which to sleep. As he stood looking straight ahead, I caught sight of the car in the distance coming to get me. This, I told him. He motioned to leave. But before doing so, he turned around and said in a low voice: "I will find a knife."

"No!" promptly shot out of my mouth and I continued insisting: "No! Not a knife, no weapon. Hear me, no weapon!" Pausing after the words, I looked directly at him and let my eyes speak volumes: "Listen to me. Understand me. Anything but a weapon."

As the car pulled into the curb, he was leaving. I was getting into the car, when he turned around once more. He said: "Have a good night," and disappeared out into the summer night.

CHAPTER 3
THE SIGNIFICANCE OF MEANING

In this chapter light is shed on how theories and pre-scientific assumptions about humanity that reduce, constrain and reify us are unreflectively being carried out as societal practice in workplaces and in educational institutions. This gives rise to an experience of being existentially threatened and an alarming number of otherwise healthy and thriving people develop anxiety, depression and traumatic stress.

As human beings, we are equipped with uniquely human preconditions that allow us to evolve physically, psychologically, emotionally, and mentally in ways that enable us to be co-creators of the very reality we inhabit. The basic human preconditions are indispensable for our sense of being human – we cannot choose to abstain from or deny these dispositions. They are fundamental aspects of being human that we need to be in touch with in order to experience ourselves – and be experienced – as healthy, viable and functioning human beings. These preconditions are essential to our perception of self and the world. Thus, the significance of experiencing meaning, coherence, perspective, and value in our everyday lives is demonstrated as being of the utmost importance for the well being and health of human beings. Seen from this perspective, the dire consequences of being dehumanized and forced to work contrary to one's professional and personal knowledge, judgment and values are pinpointed and posited as being altogether predictable.

A Sufi story is the introduction to this chapter's the field of investigation.

The overlooked subject

The smuggler, Nasrudin, arrived at the border leading a donkey laden with hay. An experienced border guard immediately spotted him. "Halt," he said, "what is your business?" "I am an honest smuggler," Nasrudin answered. "Are you?" the guard said, "then I better search those bundles of hay. If I find anything, you will have to pay duty." "Do as you please," Nasrudin replied, "but you will not find anything in the bundles." The guard closely searched through the hay, but could not find anything. Rather dissatisfied, he was forced to let Nasrudin pass over the border.

Already the next day, Nasrudin again turned up at the border with the donkey laden with hay. "This time I have to be more thorough, so that I will get him," the border guard thought to himself, and he tore the hay apart, scrutinized the donkey's harness and searched the body of Nasrudin but found nothing. Again, he was forced to let Nasrudin pass. This repeated itself, day in and day out, for years. The guard could see that Nasrudin had, in the course of time, become well dressed and that he had started to wear jewels. It was obvious that Nasrudin had become a wealthy man.

Some years later, the border guard went into retirement but he couldn't stop thinking about the man with the donkey. "I should have examined the donkey's mouth more thoroughly and perhaps even other bodily orifices," he thought. One day, the guard encountered Nasrudin at a market place and hurried over to him and said: "Tell me, my friend, if it stays between the two of us, would you please tell me what you were smuggling across the border every day for all those years?"

"Donkeys," Nasrudin answered. [45]

From time to time, we come across social scientific theories about humanity and society that initially seem to be promising and appear to illuminate our understanding of ourselves and society. But later on, the theories start to ossify in their own conceptual systems, and appears more and more to be closing up around itself, within a claustrophobic space comprised of cul-de-sacs.

Claude Lévi-Strauss and Michel Foucault – who in the 1960s represented, respectively, French philosophical structuralism and constructivism

---
45 Sufi tale, ca. 13th century. Conveyed from memory

– both advanced the view that humanity ought to be understood exclusively on the basis of collective structures – determining all thinking and behavior "behind our backs". [46] Humanity did not possess an ahistorical true nature and the death of mankind was declared. Later in life, Foucault changed his position on this reduction of humanity, stating that we carefully create ourselves as who we want be in relation to others. [47]

This does not change the fact that theories based on this mindset have been among the preferred lenses through which research and teaching within the social sciences have come to light. A great deal of research, of varying quality and varying pragmatic value, has been based on these suppositions.

Theories about the organization of work and the management strategies of the neoliberal market society have allegedly taken their points of departure in social-constructivism. This must have been appalling, to put it mildly, to critical philosophy and sociology, which have been working toward identifying and uncovering the expressions and logic of power. [48] An initially critical social-constructivist philosophy and research effort – subject to free interpretation and conceptual distortion – has thus become the very foundation for the development of management rationales and strategies whereby the general public – comprised of leaders, employees, educators and students – has been subjected to regimentation, assessment, and strict controls and has fallen victim to systematic attitude programming. [49]

The German philosopher and sociologist, Jürgen Habermas, perceives sociology from the perspective of linguistic theory – the theory of communicative action. [50] Habermas's vision is a society in which communication replaces the medium of management of the market, that is to say, money and power. Habermas makes a point of exposing the reifying and alienating system-ruled rationales of the market. However, the linguistic, abstract, and logically rational formalization of discourse suggested by Habermas runs the risk of marginalizing the subjective perspective of the individual. Thus, the theory could very well be perceived as alienating by the subjects that are supposedly taking part in the very discourses but might come to feel left out and being seen as abstractions. [51]

---

46 Foucault, 1966
47 Foucault, 1984
48 Skjervheim, 2000
49 Lauritzen, 2011
50 Habermas, 1996
51 Husserl (1962) cf., e.g. Edmund Husserl's critique of the notion of the systematic and abstract representation of life, whereby human beings are reduced to objects while the subjective capacity to interpret and systematize the steady flow of experience is overlooked.

Other researchers within critical social-scientific theory and philosophy, for instance, proponents of relationism, have expressed their critique of the reification of the subject – i.e. human beings – in our society. [52] For ideological reasons, critical social sciences also reject perceiving the subject-object relation as a power relation. Instead, the mutuality of this relation is emphasized. [53] Nonetheless, there is a risk of objectifying and reifying the subject when constantly speaking *about the subject* and when determining the subject on the basis of abstract concepts without letting the subject examine and express her- or himself. Thereby, the subject can very well be overlooked and estranged from him or herself.

The assumption of humanity's inner alienation is stated explicitly by the philosopher of dialogue, Martin Buber. Accordingly, he assumes that there is a life-conditioning tension existing in relation to the reality with which humanity is confronted and interacts in – and an inner estrangement that apparently cannot be overcome. Buber, however, perceives the dialogical space of the "I –Thou" relation – being in the totality of reality – as the suspension of estrangement.

A radically different approach to the dissolution of externally determined alienation and inner estrangement can be found in the philosophical traditions that have been developed within certain Indian scholastic traditions in the centuries following the dawn of the Christian era. One example of this is the Buddhist Madhyamika philosophy that was developed by Nargarjuna, a renowned Indian scholar and practitioner. Nargarjuna was a teacher at the Nalanda University – one of the hubs of philosophical exploration and debate at the time. [54] By applying both logical reasoning and introspective analyses and contemplation, it was demonstrated that inner estrangement and alienation are acquired and are caused by mental constructs and conceptualizations created by an "I" that is ignorant of its own true nature. The gradual letting go of and dissolution of concepts and mental constructs provides an opening into an original timeless and concept-free aware, knowing, and compassionate presence. Thus, the true nature of mind – of I and of phenomena – is, according to the knowledge espoused by this tradition, void of conceptual determination.

---

52 Lukács, 1923. The concept of reification was developed by Hungarian Marxist Georg Lukács. Honneth, 2008. According to Axel Honneth, reification is the leitmotif of social and cultural critique
53 Buber, 1997. Martin Buber underpins this social critique with an ethical and moral philosophical critique of reification
54 Nagarjuna, 2008; Jamgon Kontrul Lodro Thaye, 2007

The question is whether avoiding reification in the description of humanity and human relationships is possible. It could be argued that such a description will necessarily have to take its point of departure in our own experiences and reflections and will necessarily have to be based on first-person singular utterances. And even then, it is worth considering that we, in any case, always are already conceptualizing the subject. That is, as long as we uphold the dualistic distinction between "I" and the other.

Normative assumptions and scientific incapacitation

Basic assumptions about humanity – whether they be explicitly stated or not – will inevitably influence the knowledge that is acquired through research. There is, however, also a tendency for research results to further and reinforce pre-scientific assumptions. Thus, assumptions about humanity are not merely normative in relation to research strategy, theory formation and methodology, but can also become normative and determining factors when research is translated into concrete reality. [55]

An example is the scientifically based diagnostic construction - coined Common Mental Disorders (CMD) - that covers present-day mental ailments like anxiety, depression and stress – ailments that can be predicted as a consequence of work-related psychosocial pressure. [56] The application of the category, Common Mental Disorders, is noteworthy: it appears in various scientific studies, exploring for instance, employees on long-term sick leave and it has been applied without paying any heed to the differences between the diseases and the causes of the diseases. [57] Furthermore, using the term "Common" conveys an impression of normality: the rate of citizens who are suffering from CMD is reported to be 10-15%, and is increasing rapidly. This serves to give credence to the notion that these disorders are becoming more "ordinary" than we normally assume. Also, categorizing the ailments as "common" elicits the impression that the diseases could be said to be quite harmless. However, patients suffering from these diseases often have records of long-term sick leave and an increasing number of them never regain their ability to work.

From my own studies and my own work as a psychologist and supervisor in the field of work-related mental disorders, I have found that psychosocial stressors in the workplace and educational institutions can

---

[55] See Israel, J., 1972, 1999; Israel, S.B., 2011
[56] Stansfeld, Candy, 2006
[57] Andersen, Nielsen, Brinkmann, 2014

cause symptoms that are identical to symptoms found in patients suffering from PTSD – including symptoms of anxiety and depression, to name but a few. [58] What is also indicated is that psychosocial stressors, in severe cases, are experienced neurobiologically and mentally as an assault. This might lead to justifying the application of medication and cognitive therapy in the treatment of a growing number of imbalances that hits people today, indiscriminately.

The drugs in question and the cognitive methods can be highly relevant in the treatment of certain specific states of mental illnesses, for instance, serious depression and borderline-conditions. It appears highly questionable, however, that an alarming number of ordinary and otherwise thriving persons who quite predictably succumb to psychosocial pressures and to the imbalances of the times seem to fall outside our concepts of normality. Hence, they are running the risk of being misdiagnosed, improperly treated, and inappropriately medicated because they have been categorized as being mentally ill.

Disempowerment of citizens occurrs when healthy people who happen to be suffering from passing psychological imbalances arising in connection with serious pressures in their work and in their lives, are being forced to accept medication. There is, furthermore, a risk of arbitrarily categorizing people in the role of patients when therapists and other qualified professionals neglect to listen to these people's individual experiences. Once they succumb to the role of a patient, these people may either perish or fight tooth and nail to break free. In the case of the latter scenario, they risk suffering the disgrace that their efforts at emancipation – for instance, when they refuse to be medicated – are being construed as a lack of responsibility or willingness to cooperate. This practice toward people in our society constitutes an enormous but apparently unrecognized ethical problem that may have dire consequences for those who are subjected to it, as well as for society on the whole.

Crazy or normal?

It seems quite incomprehensible that antidepressants and depression therapy are being prescribed as the only supposedly evidence-based method of getting people back to work as soon as possible when stress breakdowns are said to be due to overly heavy work load and impossible tasks. The repeated allegation that employees who succumb to stress are too ambitious and perfectionist, is very likely a reason for not investigating too deeply into the work conditions.

---

58 Praetorius, 2007

Ask yourself however, where it leaves workers who have tried their very best to fulfill too many and at times conflicting tasks when nobody at the workplace, either at an early stage – prior to the breakdown – or subsequent to the breakdown, even bothers to place a question mark beside the adverse effects of the working conditions.

> *A large number of cases from my own psychological practice demonstrate that stress breakdown among employees are attributed – not to impossible working conditions - but to specific personal dispositions of the workers. One of these cases involved the referral for treatment of a municipal financial manager. The referral came from one of the newly formed Danish regional municipalities in 2007 and concerned one of its leading managers. She had been headhunted because her extraordinary qualifications for the position. In the months after the widespread fusion of the nation's municipalities, she succumbed to serious stress after working around the clock in response to the complete chaos prevailing in the municipal accounts and also impacting the salary and wages payroll systems. The new IT-systems were not yet fully operational and she fielded many complaints from managers, employees and the general public.*
>
> *She was referred for psychiatric treatment by the regional government's administrative manager with the expressed assignment of learning 'how to refrain from being such a perfectionist'. What was the most stressful thing to my client by far, however, was not the bizarre fact that she, as financial manager, could ever be thought of as being too much a perfectionist – what corporation or public enterprise would ever wish for a financial manager who was not meticulous to a perfectionist's degree? The real stress factor, apart from the enormous quantities of overtime she spent at the job, was the fact that she had been sworn to secrecy regarding the software's commissioning difficulties. This meant she was forced to be silent about the real causes of the errors and instead take full responsibility for all the deficiencies.*

Medicinal and therapeutic treatment of transient psychic imbalances apparently occurs without traceable interest in comprehensive knowledge about people and their work and life conditions in our times. The acquisition of necessary and relevant insight and knowledge, however, presupposes a coordinated cooperation between a wide range of mutually bordering scientific fields, theories and therapeutic schools.

If this be of any interest, that is.

At present, it seems the research activities that win the race coming in first with simple, so-called "evidence-based" research results (often based on the correlation of quantitative studies) are assigned the most prestige and attract the most substantial funds. Apparently, this practice is not affected by the fact that stress and stress-related physical and mental illnesses have been increasing, steadily, despite the fact that research within this field has received enormous grants.

It is tempting to ask: in *whose* interest does this happen? And what has become of the person, whom this is all about, in the meantime?

Consequences of scientific lapses
Along with the ongoing technological developments, sophisticated research methodologies and techniques have also been developed. The question is whether the enormous amount of collected information about humanity and society contributes to our comprehension of – and concern about – *who we are* as human beings and human societies.

The person thus seems to disappear in calculations of quantitative assessments, evaluations, and control measures. With contemporary economic pragmatism as a frame of reference, human beings are increasingly regarded as 'things' that can be quantified and modified. This is evident not only in the way people are perceived and regulated from the outside. In fact, more and more people – under the influence of externally determined reification – submit to and adapt their self-perception to the new standards of evaluation. The way is consequently paved for being manipulated into being "the quick fix", so as to be able to manage the challenges we are supposedly facing. Apparently, a growing number of people are becoming addicted to fulfilling this function as they succumb to this double fix.

The question is whether we – in sync with the construction of new interchangeable snapshots of and narratives about who we are and what makes us suitable as human beings – are on the verge of overwriting what we understand about being human. Are we, in other words, in the process of withdrawing so far from what fundamentally characterizes us as human beings that we are running the risk of eliminating ourselves altogether?

It is considerations like these that cause me to think of Georg's forest.

Georg's forest

We first had to walk the short distance from the house to the woods – then we were there! My nearly five-year-old grandchild, Georg, sought out a good branch, which fit well into his hand and was solid enough to serve him as his sword. Now the forest was his.

He ran around, merrily, poking at the dried leaves, the fallen branches, and the semi-wilted small plants on the forest floor. But suddenly, it became serious. "I am the lord of the forest, and now you shall die!" he exclaimed, while pounding away at a small young tree, only a little higher than himself. When he continued on with his ominous battle cry directed toward yet another small tree, I tried to stop him: "You can't hit the small trees because you'll ruin them. They have to grow up and become as big as the highest trees in the forest."

Completely in his own world, he continued undauntedly jumping from one tree to the next. Exerting all his power, he continued doling out blow after blow to the trees, accompanied by cries that resounded triumphantly into the woods. "No, stop it!" I yelled, "The trees are our friends. They are our breath. The forests are the world's lungs, making oxygen so we can breathe. We have to protect them." I believed I had succeeded in trumping the issue with an irresistible argument and that it would make him abruptly stop and change allegiance in favor of the trees.

But no.

Georg gathered all his powers for one last decisive and paralyzing attack. Then he rushed forward, with his sword raised high, and doled out blow after blow to each and every small tree standing in his way, while he, at the top of his voice, triumphantly proclaimed: "I am the lord of the forest. I rule the forest. And in my forest, there are no trees!"

After a short burst of surprised laughter, I had to realize that I was speechless, checkmated. Yes, even more than that. In a split second's **imperceptible changing of the rules of language and conventionally ac**cepted conceptualizations, Georg had succeeded in leaving me with a **feeling of having been unhinged from the very reality I had hitherto believed we shared.**

Naturally, I could quickly deflect the momentary experience of bewilderment that the unforeseen confrontation between two imagined realities – Georg's and my own – had brought forth. But I could not deny it.

Reality converted into language games
Can Georg's forest be said to be an emblem of the absurdities we face every day in a society that constantly confronts us with conceptual constructions and language usage which whimsically creates new conventions of meaning and converts reality into language games and narrative constructs? Does power over the means of expression create authoritative and binding perceptions of reality – without any concern about their messages being mutually exclusive – and over which we have no influence? And are we busy denying that this shakes our confidence in the reality in which we live and in our own judgment?

What happens to us, when, for instance, while tuning in on the evening news, we are told by economists and politicians that it is our responsibility as citizens to lift the country out of the economic crisis by increasing our consumption instead of saving up our resources? When we are asked to contribute to the growth of societal production and spend our money freely, while we, at the same time, are facing the prospects of a decline in real wages and an increase in prices? In a time marked by uncertainty, where it cannot be taken for granted that we can forever count on keeping our jobs and being able to pay our fixed expenses. A time in which more and more unskilled people as well as well-educated people are already being forced out of their homes due to long-term unemployment and who – together with a whole generation of young unemployed – run the risk of having to occupy a long-term position on the lowest rungs of the social ladder.

In a TV-program following the news broadcast, on the very same evening, we are informed by clear figures and knowledgeable arguments that we, in the near future, can expect a shortage of commodities and energy on a scale we can hardly imagine. That we, within a few years, due to the world-wide shortage of energy and raw materials, are going to be forced to reduce consumption of what we today consider indispensable goods. And already now, we are being advised to lower our consumption and scrap our "use and throw away" mentality and to think more along the lines of durability.

In disbelief at this clash of double messages, we ask ourselves: "What are they *talking* about?"

The unruly reality

Depending on our temperament, we may choose to simply throw the towel into the ring – for instance, by refusing to deal with it or by denying having heard this. And we may choose to enclose ourselves in, around ourselves – just like the theoretical constructs surrounding us and molding our way of perception. Or else, we become cynical and look after ourselves at the expense of others in the struggle for survival. Or each of us as individuals may choose to construct homemade opinions as a kind of protection, shielding us off from the world – a world where the creation of reality results in a chaotic mixture of intended and unintended consequences of abstract reality constructs combined with technological enterprise - constructs that simultaneously define us as human beings.

Are we affected by this – or perhaps even shaken to our core? In such a case, anxiety-reducing drugs and antidepressants or performance enhancers can help us stay on track in the pursuit of long-term objectives that are increasingly fading out of sight.

The absence of thoughtfulness, of knowledge of human nature, and of ethical considerations in these juggling determinations of reality becomes increasingly clearer when we consider the man-made consequences of this quandary. The question is, how long we can endure denying that we are confronted by growing human deprivation and suffering as well as by a planet that is slowly but surely being drained of all that is the precondition for preservation of life. And how long can we continue to deny that we are not only facing rather straightforward practical challenges but also yet another gigantic ethical challenge, which is becoming harder to ignore day by day?

The responsibility for basic sanity

Maybe we – rather sooner than later – are going to have to come to terms with a situation in which we are left to our own devices. Where we have to come to grips with the fact that finding meaning, perspective and direction cannot be left to others and where we – in order to avoid being consumed by a sense of total impotence – are going to have to shoulder a joint responsibility for (re)establishing the contact to something fundamentally healthy and true about being human.

Consciously taking responsibility for making existential choices and putting them into practice presuppose that we are willing to refrain from denying the powerlessness brought about by reification and dehumanization in our time. In other words, we need to initiate a process of emancipation whereby we, with increased clear-sightedness and awareness, reconsider what we as human beings are actually capable of. Not to assert ourselves as a counterforce and not to exert energy and power on standing in opposition but rather to point out entirely new avenues paved with fundamentally different ways of thinking, acting and being in the world.

Blind confidence in actors outside us and higher up in the social hierarchy is going to have to be counterbalanced by participation in movements in which every one of us is at liberty to take responsibility. Where we, through a joint effort can emancipate ourselves and actively take part in encountering the challenges of our time.

This might sound like idealistic and overheated oration, but what is the alternative to becoming co-creators of a world which, in its dynamic and continual unfurling – overall and all along – might make sense to ourselves and others? A world in which each of us assumes the responsibility for contributing, in thought, speech and action, to uncovering and emancipating potentials in ourselves as individuals and social communities that may turn out to be crucial to the continuance of human existence on Earth.

The existential point of departure

In the following, we will focus on the human potentials that we need to mature in order for emancipation to take place. The point of departure is existential philosophy and psychology. A description will be given of a way of perceiving some basic preconditions that characterize what it is to be human. [59] Basic preconditions that are considered to be universal to humanity, which are ripened and expressed in the life of human beings, in ongoing interaction with biological processes and dispositions, with the brain's development and function, and with the surrounding social community. The underlying assumption is that every single human being – depending on his or her individual dispositions - is capable of assuming a central role in her/his own life and in mutually dependent relations with others as an outgrowth of the innately human capacity to reflect and think rationally, empathically and creatively.

---

59 Arendt, 1978. What we may understand by basic conditions are described and designated in different ways within contemporary philosophy. Hannah Arendt speaks of the fundamental activities our faculties: (1) thinking, (2) willing, and (3) judging or using our judgment.

Basic human preconditions

Human beings are – like other living creatures on Earth – equipped with drives and instinctual abilities that make it possible to live and survive as individuals and as a species. As human beings, however, we are equipped with uniquely human preconditions that allow us to evolve physically, psychologically, emotionally, and mentally in ways that enable us to be co-creators of the very reality we inhabit. Thus we can consciously choose the fundamental values, norms, attitudes and customs that become valid for the individual and valid with respect to relationships within the communities we create.

The basic preconditions that make us human and that distinguish us from other living beings are fundamental activities and qualities like for instance awareness, thinking, reflection and self-reflection, empathy, compassion, creativity, joy, will power, love and humor. Our being-in-the-world can thus be seen as a potentially creative and interminable expression of qualities, the maturation and expression of which can be observed from the outside. At the same time, these fundamental activities and qualities can be observed as inner experiences having specific experiential qualities that make it possible to differentiate between them. [60]

It is perhaps awareness, thinking, reflection, self-reflection, and empathy that primarily distinguish human beings from other living creatures. It is through these activities that we are able to know about ourselves, the world and the people around us. We can also experience and sense what occurs within ourselves and inside others. We are even aware of our own awareness and knowledge. Apart from accumulating information and knowledge, we are also able to become wiser and to create knowledge when our experiences and empathy are combined with our ability to think rationally, insightfully and creatively.

The life and development of humanity are – in a historical perspective – not merely questions of perpetually adapting, adjusting, exploring and creating new ways of securing our biological survival but also have to do with our ability to create new knowledge. This has been vital in the formation and development of human communities, ways of life and

---

[60] Basic human preconditions, e.g., human qualities and potentials, are intangible, the "existence" of which cannot be delimited and described as something substantial and measurable. With the help of a metaphor from modern physics, the same is the case when dealing with particles and black matter in the universe, the existence-form of which is transient or cannot be described.

cultures. [61] Communities and cultures which, to us, are as important as breathing the air around us and obtaining nourishment.

However, the altogether unique thing about us as human beings is that we are equipped with the ability to explore what it means to be human. Awareness, thinking, reflection, self-reflection, introspection and empathy are among the altogether unique human potentials by means of which we perceive and are aware of a multitude of levels of consciousness, mind and reality formation. Perhaps we are prone to taking this for granted but it is actually exceptional and provides us with the opportunity – and we might add, the responsibility – to consciously develop and mature as the human beings we have the potential to be. This applies to inner and deeper existential levels of mind and being as well as to how we develop, in the outer common reality, as individuals and members of communities.

Our human potentials are reflected in the make-up and function of the brain. Just like animals, we are equipped with centers at the back of the brain that ensure our biological survival, centers that support instinctual abilities and automatic mechanisms of reaction and behavior. In addition to this, human beings are equipped with centers at the front and the central parts of the brain, the makeup and function of which are preconditions for our thinking, feeling, being aware and managing ourselves and our lives, and for maturing as a person and as a fellow human being.

Given these basic preconditions, human development, expression and existence are characterized by what, for the species, is a remarkably extensive flexibility and freedom to choose to express one's potentials according to her/his intentions and ideas about what life as a human being involves. This being said, there are certain conditions that seem to have to be fulfilled for human beings to live and express themselves in a healthy, viable and functional way. We will elucidate this in the following sections.

Meaning, coherence, perspective, and value

Among the more complex and higher functions of the human potential is our ability to experience meaning, coherence, and perspective – both in the present moment and in existence in its entirety. We are not concerned here with experiencing some kind of meaning with life or with whether any specific purpose about life is assumed. The point here is that life and existence *give* meaning in the sense of *an experience of meaningfulness*. The experience of meaning, coherence and perspective

---
61 Deacon, 1997; Mithen, 1996

is inextricably linked to the experience of value, as such, as well as being linked to the experience of value as an individual human being and as a member of social communities.

The basic human preconditions are indispensable for our sense of being human – we cannot choose to abstain from or deny these dispositions. They are fundamental aspects of being human that we *need* to be in touch with in order to experience ourselves – and be experienced – as healthy, viable and functioning human beings. These preconditions are essential to our perception of self and the world.

It is, in other words, of the utmost importance that we acknowledge that our mental and emotional health rests on the following conditions:

1. That we, without hindrances, can develop and use our uniquely human capacity to think, reflect and be empathic.

2. That we experience meaning, coherence, perspective and a sense of value in our lives. (18)

That is to say, if our ability to think, reflect, and empathize is hindered, and if our experience of meaning, coherence, perspective and sense of value is threatened, we will be shaken to our core. We will – in the event that the hindrance or threat continues over a longer period of time and we are unable to change the situation – experience a loss of control of ourselves and a loss of our mental and emotional health. In the final instance, we will feel threatened – and not only with regard to meaning, perspective and value. Also, our self-confidence, our perception of reality and our personal integrity will start to crumble. In reality, we will feel that our lives are being existentially threatened, whether we are aware of this or not. [62]

Findings from recent neuroscience suggest that regardless of whether we feel threatened in a biological or an existential sense, the brain will register this as if we were standing in a life-threatening situation. The brain's reaction is the same in either case, that is to say, there is no distinction made between an existential and a biological life-threatening situation. As described in Chapter 2, the areas of the brain that are normally activated in dangerous situations will not only dominate the brain function: they will also suppress the centers of the higher mental and

---

62 This will be elaborated in Chapter 4, where the effects of externally determined alienation and dehumanizing – and the consequent violation of the experience of meaning – will be elucidated

emotional functions. This will in turn cause us to further lose contact with our ability to think clearly and coherently, and accordingly, we will lose confidence in our own sense perceptions, our empathy, our judgment, and our experience of reality.

An everyday and harmless example of a sudden loss of orientation occurs when walking down a flight of stairs and finding, without advance notice, that a step is "missing". This will be registered by the brain and trigger off a neurobiological activation, as though we were in danger. The mild and momentary state of shock will, in a split second, promptly be followed by our realization that we *thought* the stairs had another step. We will again experience the meaningfulness of the situation and the neurobiological high-stress condition will soon be normalized. Similarly, the brain registers danger when – during a normal conversation – what is said is suddenly utterly incomprehensible and makes no sense. It is not until the possible misunderstanding has been cleared up that the brain's state of alarm will be mollified.

During a psychological breakdown, regardless of whether it happens to be a transient state brought about by psychosocial stress, abuse or torture, or whether it is the forerunner for an actual mental illness, the experience of the loss of meaning is devastating and instigates deep anxiety. The delusions of a psychotic patient can thus be perceived as an attempt to create meaning. Regardless of how frightening the delusions might be, they are still basically a protection against the feeling of personal disintegration that are being experienced in case there is a total loss of meaning.

Physically and psychologically healthy people can also be seized by an experience of meaninglessness and worthlessness. This might happen in cases where we might be subjected to a trauma – for instance, a disaster, abuse, the loss of a close relative – or in the case of a breakdown from psychosocial stress. Nothing matters, and one's existence is experienced as bereft of meaning and value. A traumatized person is running a higher risk of developing a depression with suicidal thoughts because his or her existence becomes unbearable when this bereavement is experienced.

Making sense of meaning
Experiencing something making sense or being meaningful is not merely a mental notion or thought structure, emerging from external knowledge and information, but an inner contact with and realization of something being experienced as correct and true. We feel a sense of certainty. We have what is almost a bodily sensation of something making sense.

Something making sense or being meaningful is experienced on at least at two levels:

1) One level can be expressed verbally, as in the statement that something "makes a lot of sense". This means that something seems right, in the sense that it appears to be reasonable. An example that illustrates this is that it "makes sense" and it seems reasonable to get paid for doing a job – and that the payment ought to correspond to the effort. This view can be argued rationally and we may have an opinion about the question, an opinion that leaves room for flexibility. What could, for example, be discussed is how vast differences among different wages that we generally find will make sense, to us, and thus discuss the degree of inequality in society we are willing to accept.

2) We are experiencing yet another qualitatively different level when we speak about something making sense or being meaningful *to us*. This can be characterized by our being in contact with something that is deeply meaningful and true to us – something that lies beyond debate. An example is the statement: "All human beings are equal, regardless of whether they are poor or rich, whether they have a job or not, and regardless of religion, race, and nationality." This statement expresses an existential truth for the person voicing it. Relinquishing this truth by, for instance, being forced to view, treat or witness others treating any human being as inferior, will be experienced as deeply compromising for the person. The person's experience of retaining his or her integrity and of being true to what, for this person, constitutes a basic precondition of being human is going to be devastated.

Especially at this level of experienced meaning, a *forced* change in the definition of an opinion of something that makes sense – caused for instance, by dictate or by external demands and expectations – may yield the result that we are placed in an irresolvable double-binding situation, in which we cannot do the right thing. This shakes our perception of reality and our confidence in our own judgment. This will be further elucidated – with the use of examples – in Chapters 4 and 5.

The need for value, appreciation and belonging

The experience of meaning, coherence, and perspective and the underlying experience of value are vital to us as individuals and in our communities. The sense of value, of something being precious, is linked to feeling appreciated and to having a sense of belonging within our social communities. It is, however, essential that these communities build on shared values and norms that *make sense to us*.

If we experience a lack of personal value due to insufficient appreciation from the community that we belong to – for instance, at work – we will feel that our existence is threatened. As a consequence, crucial reference points that allow us to orient ourselves in relation to ourselves and to others in our social community are lost.

The same applies when the basic values of a society or work place are changed, and when they are openly or covertly being reinterpreted so that we can no longer be confident that:

1. We are participatory and responsible actors in communities that are based on commonly accepted and shared value.

2. We are supported and appreciated as members of a consistent, cohesive, and fundamentally meaningful community.

The survival strategies of powerlessness

If we experience being powerless because we cannot influence or change the situation we are in, we are forced to adapt ourselves to the circumstances by developing survival strategies. This may imply that we, in our thoughts and our actions, conform to and acquire a new sense of meaning and value in order to regain the necessary appreciation, nourishment, and acceptance and to avoid being ostracized and isolated.

Through the survival strategy's adaption to external demands and expectations, we risk being cut off from our unique resources and our own authentic ways of experiencing, expressing and existing – as ourselves. The survival strategies, in other words, alienate us from ourselves and gradually fixate us in an inflexible and more or less conscious surveillance and behavior regulation of ourselves. In other words, we lose the freedom to choose to think and act authentically and we lose the freedom to be true to ourselves. [63]

---

[63] Survival strategies, their function, and their consequences will be further elucidated in Chapters 4 and 5, where inner strangeness and externally determined alienation will be the topics. What it means to experience oneself authentically will be elucidated in Chapter 5 and Chapter 6.

Existence, meaning and ethics

An indispensable aspect of being and feeling human – both individually and in relation to others – is ethical discernment. Ethical discernment operates in the mutual relation between, on the one hand, an experience of meaning and value and, on the other, a fundamental capacity of human intelligence and empathy to distinguish between good and evil, between right and wrong, and between true and false. It is these capacities for discernment that allow us to choose to act ethically, that is, for the benefit of ourselves and others, and to avoid harming ourselves and others. [64]

It is as a consequence of our present, attentive awareness being in contact with this discernment that we are capable of choosing to mature and express our human qualities and to display, for instance, empathy, compassion, creativity, will power, strength, courage, determination and love in ways that are adequate and beneficial to ourselves and to others in the life situations in which we find ourselves. This, on its part, reinforces the experience that being human is valuable and that human existence is meaningful.

It is a recurring theme in this book that the experience of meaning and the experience of the meaningfulness of being and living as a human being depend on the extent to which we can consciously and openly express our human potential for thinking, speaking and acting ethically. A consistently ethical mindset, attitude and conduct are, in other words, based on a conscious choice of investigating, developing and expressing one's human qualities in the best possible way – in order to benefit oneself and one's community. [65]

An ethical way of life furthermore implies a heightened attentiveness and awareness about what is needed in the situation as well as awareness about the obstacles – springing forth both from the outer world and from oneself – that need be overcome in order to fulfill one's wish to live as an ethical human being.

---

64 As will be expounded in Chapter 5, this empathy and discernment are already expressed in the early phase of attachment between mother and child in the child's first years.

65 This view is very much in keeping with both spiritual and humanistic ideas within Western and Eastern thought. Like other contemplative traditions of wisdom, Buddhist philosophy has evidently inspired modern philosophers like Karl Jaspers. See Zahavi, 2003.

Counteracting the dire consequences of reductionism and reification

In this chapter, it has been rendered probable that human beings, by acquiring a more comprehensive knowledge and self-awareness, based on an all-encompassing view of humanity, are going to be able to transcend the growing feeling of incapacitation and powerlessness so typical of the times. This will go hand-in-hand with actually reinstating oneself as an active and responsible participant in the creation of a meaningful reality that we can abide by – individually and communally.

For this to happen, we have to acknowledge that relying on theories and pre-scientific assumptions about humanity that reduce and reify us has devastating repercussions, especially when the theories are unreflectively implemented as societal practices.

It has been stated and demonstrated here that the significance of experiencing meaning, coherence, perspective, and value in our everyday lives is of the utmost importance for the well being and the health of human beings. Seen from this perspective, the dire consequences of reductionism and the "rational bypassing" of management within private and public sectors have been identified and established as being utterly predictable.

In the following chapters, this will be further elucidated by case studies and testimonies from workplaces, educational institutions and fields of scientific research.

CHAPTER 4
ALIENATION, STRESS AND CONFORMIST INDIVIDUALISM

A recurring theme in this chapter is that the notion of humanity that is at the root of and entrenching the neoliberal economic theory and the corresponding management measures in a very short time has been integrated by the citizens as a general perception of self and society.

By way of metaphor, it is shown that alienation occurs when, almost without sensing it, we are deprived of the experience of something intimate and original within ourselves. This implies being disconnected from the experience of value and meaning in being the person and fellow human being we are and have the potential to become.

The dire human and social consequences of this are described and documented by accounts and case-studies. What is rendered probable here is that work-related traumatic stress reaction is frequently an all-too-human response to inhumane conditions. The greatest "problem" for people who are seriously affected is that they cannot withstand working contrary to fundamental human values that make sense and that are indisputable, from their point of view. This is only further exacerbated with the emergence of a climate of untrustworthiness and deceit in the competition-ridden public and private institutions and workplaces. These dehumanizing measures are experienced as an assault on students, on teachers, on leaders, and on employees who consequently develop work-related traumatic stress – with symptoms similar to PTSD.

Out of the box – out of the closet?

A couple of years ago, I participated in a conference aimed at organizing new strategies to improve conditions in work environments and to set up goals to be reached by 2020. The participants were professionals representing labor unions, research institutions, public institutions and private companies. All participants were, in their daily jobs, engaged in leadership development, employee security, and research related to work environments and to the prevention and treatment of work-related physical and psychological diseases. We were encouraged to think "out of the box" and to allow ourselves and each other to present brand new perspectives and entirely new points of view

Before we even started, we were informed that the overall agenda was predetermined: the productivity of work and economic growth should increase in the period from now and up until 2020 in order for Denmark to be able to compete with the rest of the world.

The question is, however, whether it is possible to carry out radical changes when these are supposed to build on exactly the same lines of reasoning that brought about the problems in the first place. To think "out of the box" implies a change of discourse – which might directly or indirectly represent a critique or even a denouncement of conventionally accepted notions and ways of thinking – to which we were supposedly being given free passage. But is it so that thinking "out of the box" additionally involves the courage and the will to come "out of the closet" and seriously reflect on one's own experiences and express what gives meaning to oneself? And furthermore, to honestly admit that ones' own workplace – whether it be situated on the premises of the labor unions, of the research institutions, of the public institutions or of the private companies – is exposed to the very same conditions that send an increasing number of citizens on long-term leave due to work-related mental and physical disorders.

In the following – after the preamble of a metaphor – it will be elucidated how work conditions can cause dehumanization, which leads to disabling physical sickness and mental disorders.

A metaphor:

> *When a note is struck on an instrument, it is the overtones that tell us what instrument it is. An 'A' sounded on a cello and an 'A' sounded on a piano or on a piccolo flute have very different overtones. It is the overtones that make an instrument and its tones sound different from other instruments and make the instruments unique. This is also the case within the same category of instruments – for instance, violins. There are no two violins that are completely identical with respect to the variation and composition of their overtones.*
>
> *The unique timbre emerges in the very creation of sound – for instance, when a chord is being struck or during the passage of an air*

current through a mouthpiece. But also the material the instrument is made from, its soundboard and its resonator all contribute to creating the timbre and overtones of the tone.

To this it must be added that the atomic structure and the acoustic pattern of the instrument are altered when it is played and that the changes depend on who is playing the instrument and how.

Something similar applies to the human voice: the number and variation of overtones is different from one person to another. It is the overtones of the voice that allow us to recognize a person's voice and make it possible for us, for instance, when talking on the phone with someone whose voice we are familiar with, to take it for granted that the person in question is actually who he or she declares him- or herself to be. Also here, the primary source of sound, i.e. the vocal chords, works in close harmony with the "soundboard" and the "resonator" in creating the sound of the voice. When it comes to human beings, what we mean by 'soundboard' and 'resonator' constitutes an infinitely complex interaction between not just physical but also mental and emotional dimensions of the person's being, personality and expression.

In experiments with recordings of sound from musical instruments and the human voice where the overtones are gradually filtered out, a certain threshold-limit can be reached where we can no longer hear from which instrument the tone originates and we are not able to recognize a particular person's voice.

This was what came to mind when I was in a session, some years back, with a man who was the manager of an enterprise with many employees and users. Apart from having been assigned to reorganize the distribution of work in order to achieve greater productivity, he was also responsible for the management and development of the company's staff members. He had specifically been asked to take on the task of remedying an incredibly negative working environment.

After only a few months of working in a position for which he had been headhunted, he was in a state of work-related stress reaction. He spoke incoherently and time and time again he interrupted himself. On the whole, he appeared fragmented, anxious and restless. The man had seen a doctor in connection with having experienced heart troubles and insomnia. He exhibited a tendency toward being testy and irritable but even more awkwardly, he had become increasingly prone to crying and in some situations at the workplace, he had not been able to hold back the tears. It was extremely difficult for him to concentrate and – predictably enough, as would become apparent – to grab hold of the bigger picture of the many conflicting expectations and demands that were part and parcel of his working conditions and functions. This was especially so because his efforts and solutions in one particular area were in conflict with what might have been needed in other areas. In reality, his tasks increasingly seemed to obstruct each other and put him in an irreconcilable situation.

Personally, he believed that the problem was of his own making and as I have often experienced, the ongoing conflict between his different tasks was, according to this perspective, a conflict that was positioned within himself: he was not assertive enough and he was putting too much effort and time into seeing how the land lay and too much effort and time into being empathic - and this was paralyzing him, he believed. This is what he had been told time and time again on a leadership development course and by the company's CEO. The agenda of his superior in sending this man to see me turned out to be simple and clear: I was supposed to give him a swift kick in the pants and coach him so that he could cut through all the complaints and give the staff some proper leadership.

My impression of the man was that he – much like many others suffering from stress reactions – had lost his footing in himself. He was fleeing from himself and was in the process of writing off some his most precious qualities. In spite of his condition, it was not difficult to sense that behind all the current symptoms of a stress reaction, this man possessed an obvious talent for leadership – he was capable of combining rational analysis with empathy and adept at communicating and inspiring confidence in the staff. However, it could also be seen that he, in keeping with the advent of modern, economically determined management strategies, had increasingly taken it upon himself to adapt to and identify with concepts, language use and attitudes that were being created and continuously developed by whatever the currently prevailing management-geared thinking happened to be.

My proposal was completely the opposite of his own, namely that he needed a "time out", in which he could retrieve the tools to curb his condition of mental and emotional chaos. And I shared my knowledge with him that he, like most people with an acute stress reaction, was experiencing a very painful condition that invariably sets in when we, due to unbearable external pressure, feel overwhelmed, powerless, and cut off from our familiar selves. And I suggested to him that his brain was in a pent-up neurobiological state of high stress, as if he were in a life-threatening situation.

Whenever I talk to people who are suffering from a high stress condition and call their attention to the fact that what they need most of all is to come "home" to – and feel – themselves, the reaction is an admixture of relief and being moved. The person typically experiences a deep longing to get in touch with him- or herself and to gain insight into his or her condition, so that *something* can be done about it. Not seldom the eyes moisten ... and sometimes the tears flow, unchecked.

To my great surprise, my client the manager, reacted by showing a genuine interest in my "observation". "Really?" he said, and continued inquiring about what screws could be turned so that he could improve his competence of being in contact with himself.

In the course of the following sessions, and in tandem with the rehabilitation program's balancing of his nervous system, the attachment to and identification with the reifying management rhetoric was gradually supplanted by his own words and experiences. Also, the standardized conceptualization he had of himself as a human being was replaced by a growing recognition of – and becoming – the person he used to be.

It is at *this* point that a deeper rehabilitation of a person can begin.

The alienated human being

The sense of alienation that pervades a person who is deprived of, or who renounces contact with crucial aspects or qualities in themselves, can be compared to the instrument or the voice that has been filtered of its overtones. The intimate relationship between the voice and the soundboard and resonator of the voice is severed, causing the expressiveness and the sound of the voice to be reduced beyond recognition. The tone of the voice – detached from its origin – is a perfect and freely floating vibration, the frequency of which can easily be registered with computerized measurements; its graphic image can actually be seen on a screen as a simple and predictably progressing sine wave.

The records of the computerized control and the management tools that have become immensely popular in workplaces, and by which the effectiveness and goal achievements of the employees are continuously controlled, observed and assessed, can be seen as a parallel to this. In order to achieve a quantitative measurement of the employee's performance, standardized parameters have to be used that are the same for everybody and apply to everybody, regardless of the fact that the various employees' situations are different. The qualities that employees display while performing their jobs – not to mention the quality of the work in question – are not taken into account, regardless of how much is being uttered back and forth about "quality management".

This not only influences how the work performance is being assessed: it will also affect the way that employees assess themselves and shape their professional and personal self-perception and integrity. The employee is taught to view him- or herself through the eyes of others – that is, to perceive him or herself in the light of the continuously changing, labor-market relevant perspective of the workplace. The surveillance and control to which the employee is subjected appear opaque, inasmuch as there is neither a manager nor another co-worker who is personally looking over the employee's shoulder and reporting on him or her. The employee reports on and potentially informs on him- or herself, on the basis of a computerized and standardized notion of what the workplace is presumed to expect and demand, a notion that the employee tries to identify with. It is on the background of the data that the employee feeds into the software that the overall assessment and control are subsequently carried out.

Alienation and inner homelessness

When a person is alienated from their own self by virtue of having to identify with and assess themself on the basis of externally determined measures of productivity and performance, they run the risk of being dissociated from an authentic and direct contact with their own qualities. They are no longer directly accessible because they have become targeted so that they fit the software's parameters for the self-reporting. The person also risks developing a deficiency in the contact with his or her own ground and unique soundboard and with his or her own physical, mental, and spiritual spaces of expression.

In order to understand - and hence disentangle the suffering of being reduced as an individual person - it is important to examine externally determined alienation: Externally determined alienation is the process that takes place when a person adapts to, internalizes and identifies with the reifying perspective of the environment. Eventually, an externally determined alienation results in an inner estrangement.

Alienation that is brought about by dehumanization occurs when we, almost without sensing it, are deprived of experiencing something intimate and original in ourselves that is connected to the experience of meaning and the truth of essentially being the person and fellow human being we are – and have the potential to be.

To be alienated is to be homeless – to be *out of oneself*.

The fragile identity formation of alienation

If a person's experience of identity and self-perception is not adequately based on an inner and attentive contact with his or her own qualities, then the person will primarily have to rely on notions and opinions obtained from the surrounding environment. The perceptions of self and of the world are thus deposited in the consciousness as abstract mental formations, which are only vaguely grounded in the person's own inner experiences. The upshot of this is the development of a superficial, fragile and inadequate experience of identity. The externally determined self-images will – qua superficial and replaceable mental formations – invariably contribute, in the course of time, to an experience of inner emptiness and a more or less recognizable feeling of being insignificant. It is also possible that a kind of mental blindness and a sense of disinterest in and lack of empathy with oneself and others can set in.

A person who develops a distorted and inauthentic personality as a consequence of externally determined alienation becomes insecure with regard to feeling and determining the quality of his/her own presence. The person suffers from a lack of confidence in being able to discern and judge. He or she will therefore come to crave external affirmation and recognition as a substitute for the inner sense of certainty about and confidence in his or her own worth and value.

The limitation that sets in with regard to the individual's personality development and self-expression has – as will be described in Chapter 5 – features in common with the consequences of an authoritarian upbringing in which the child's personal space is invaded and undermined. This leaves not only the child but also the adult submitted to this in a situation in which he or she, on basis of the resultant dependency on the authority figure, is forced to submit in order to gain acceptance and avoid exclusion. Both the child and the adult are brought into a complex situation in which the person has to haggle to maintain the (vitally) necessary sense of belonging and gain rewards in return for adapting to a situation-relevant personality.

Basic confidence in oneself and the environment is a foundation upon which we feel encouraged to explore, discover and establish a sense of ourselves and the world. However, the basic trust that might be developed in early childhood is not established once and for all. Reifying management practices, such as conducting quality controls by means of quantitative methods of documentation and self-reporting, present the risk of estranging a person from him or herself and thereby undermine the experience of basic trust. These types of management and assessment tools, having gained greater prevalence within the spheres of education and management – from the childcare of early infants through educational institutions to workplaces – have to be considered a serious assault on a healthy and continued development of basic trust and hence on human beings' opportunities to develop and mature fully.

The application of reifying and of cognate dehumanizing learning and management methods seems to rely on a blatant ignorance about how human beings are actually capable of developing and expressing their potentials and qualities, fully – this is an ignorance that contributes to an unhealthy dehumanization and to the proliferation of human beings' alienation in our day.

The relation between dehumanization, alienation, and stress

If we wish to understand some central causal connections that can be correlated with the explosive increase of stress-related mental imbalances and disorders, it is essential that we take into account that we, as human beings, react – neurobiological, physically and psychologically – as though we were being subjected to abuse when we are forced to identify with and express norms, attitudes, and values that are incompatible with fundamental aspects of being human. The same applies in instances where we are deprived of the experience of meaning in situations in which we find ourselves. To be estranged from oneself may thus, in serious cases, trigger a traumatic reaction. In Chapter 3, it was emphasized how crucial it is for our mental and emotional health that we are given opportunities to use our human capacity to think, to reflect and to be empathic. Furthermore, it is vital for us that our experience of the situation we are in and the way we relate to it *make sense*.

Changing our minds can be appropriate and doing so may be a sign of flexibility when new information makes such a change of mind relevant and when it generally feels right. But when a person is forced by decree to change his or her attitude to the human values that make sense to the person and have fundamental significance to his or her understanding of him/herself and the meaningfulness and value of existence, changing one's mind can be associated with a loss of confidence in one's own experience of reality and judgment. Perhaps it is worth reflecting on the fact that such coercion-based techniques, when employed during psychological torture, undermine the person's judgment, discernment, and experience of meaning and value, and that these constitute a sure way of undermining the person, psychologically, and eventually causing a psychological breakdown.

Even though the degrees and variations of this kind of undermining can rightly be said to vary, the price that a person who is subjected to this treatment has to pay will nevertheless be that the person can be forced to deny or cut off contact with fundamental and sense-making values. The person will then have to endure a condition of not being true to him/herself.

This can happen, for example, when employees, in the name of productivity and competitiveness, are burdened with workloads that exceed the capacity of the individuals, and when professionally competent reasoning and constructive solutions that these employees might contribute are misconstrued as being disloyal and untimely complaints that may even trigger the issuing of a pink slip. As a consequence of this, a work culture is being created in which employees and leaders almost imperceptibly learn to conform to and integrate a new collective perception of reality within their personal perceptions of themselves and the world.

Such a culture was gradually introduced in the 1990s, when contemporary private and public forms of organization and management were implemented in a sweeping wave of structural changes. As an important motivating factor in the employees' compulsory acceptance of the changed conceptual framework around work and education, three specific claims were featured, which came to fashion the basis for the new collective perception of self and the world:

1. Until now, we have not been good enough.
2. We have to become better.
3. We have to compete to become the best (in the world).

The first wave of serious work-related stress-reaction that appeared some 10-15 years ago among employees who were working at public-sector jobs and for private enterprises was largely due to excessive workloads. It primarily affected the employees who had not yet realized that they were unable to perform tasks with the same professional attitude and the same sense of responsibility that they were accustomed to and that they had trained for doing. Even if today, excessive workloads are still the most commonly mentioned cause of stress, this is, at the same time, the most easily addressed and easily tackled problem in stress prevention and the rehabilitation of stress reactions.

It is, however, quite a different matter in cases of more serious stress factors and the matching stress reactions.[66] Among more serious stress factors number, for example, impossible working conditions, in which the work cannot be carried out in a qualified way and/or in a manner that makes sense. Also included among the more serious stress factors are situations in which one, as a leader or an employee, is caught in an out-and-out double-bind situation, where no matter what the individual in question does, it will *always* be wrong and where this person is subsequently held responsible for flaws and defects.

The same applies to the reifying application of work manuals and the progressively ruthless regimentation of employees as well as to the introduction of "quality control", replete with assorted time-consuming and absurd self-reporting and assessment measures and demands for the fulfillment of contractual goals that are impossible to achieve within the given financial and temporal framework.

When employees are subjected to unreasonable and impossible contracts drawn up for the purpose of securing greater profits and thereby better bottom-line results, we have to assume that the manager has very limited knowledge about the employees' sphere of competence. Or that the manager, in order to maintain his or her managerial position, is handling the management functions in accordance with an overall financial objective and is leaving it to the hired employees to deal with the impossible situations themselves.

For this purpose, a management language has been developed that, by utilizing quickly replaceable catch-phrases like "self-management", "value-based and appreciative management", "employee involvement", "employee responsibility" and "taking ownership", makes it look like the employee has a real influence on the performance of his or her job. And this travesty is articulated in the jargon of management newspeak, the purpose of which is to give the employees and the management the impression 1) that the management, organization and framework around the job performance have been arranged so that the employees can count on the best possible working conditions, and 2) that the employees can have faith in their efforts being respected and appreciated. It

---

66 Praetorius, N.U. (2004, 2007)

stands to reason, then, that it is consequently the employee's own fault if problems occur in connection with carrying out the performance of tasks or if the employee does not thrive under the given circumstances.

The aforementioned stress factors, in combination, effectively undermine a person's professional and personal integrity. This process manifests itself in the employee's becoming insecure, losing self-esteem, and doubting his or her judgment and qualifications for the job. In serious cases, the person might develop a serious stress reaction, depression and anxiety.

A frightening feeling of being alien to oneself, of no longer knowing oneself, and of not being able to do what one has been used to doing are common symptoms that are suffered by a severely stressed person. In such a case, the person might be suffering from anxiety, depression, mood swings, memory failure and concentration problems, sleep disorders, restlessness, and hyperactivity, succeeded in some cases by attendant feelings of powerlessness, deep fatigue and even paralysis.

Self-perpetuating estrangement
To be subjected to externally determined alienation as a consequence of being over-taxed and reduced to a self-supervising instrument in the production of quantifiable goals is existentially devastating to a person – as when the overtones are gradually filtered away from the sound of an instrument or from the human voice. It becomes registered in our neurobiological system, as if we were in a life-threatening situation. The brain function is thus – should the condition be inescapable and become permanent – in a chronic neurobiological state of high stress. The brain function that is normally activated in dangerous situations – performed by the lower instinctual centers – will tend to suppress activity that would otherwise be transpiring in the centers of the higher functions. In other words, the functioning of the centers that enable us to use the uniquely human abilities such as thinking, intelligent discernment, reflection, self-reflection, creativity, empathy, and compassion is impeded. This, on its part, reinforces the sense of being cut off from oneself, of being strange to oneself.

A self-perpetuating vicious spiral emerges, in which being subjected to externally determined alienation can give rise to a chronic state of stress. The person is increasingly losing control and the feeling of being alien to oneself is thus being reinforced, so to speak, from inside the person. The ability to make judgments is impaired and the person becomes incapable of making relevant decisions. The person, who increasingly thinks and acts as if he or she were running on autopilot, will continue on the disastrous and apparently inevitable course, heading toward an actual stress-collapse or burnout.

Depression and stress

Lack of recognition of the nature and complexity of work-related stress factors may be accountable for the failure to prevent severe stress conditions and to reduce the number of burnout- and stress-related disorders. Furthermore, it appears that stress treatment does not seem to be particularly successful over time; this is presumably due to a lack of knowledge about the psychic and neurobiological conditions of stress. A growing number of relapses after the treatment of severe work-related stress reactions can thus be observed. According to several studies, the number of people that do not return to work after taking sick leave because of stress and stress-related physical imbalances is also on the rise. [67] The manner of diagnosing work-related stress seems to play a crucial role in this predicament, inasmuch as there is a widespread tendency to confer the diagnosis of "depression" on stress patients and overlook what might actually be triggering the stress reaction.

That it is tempting to use the diagnosis of "depression" in cases of stress reactions can probably be related to the fact that depression and stress reaction, according to the common classifications of these diagnoses, display almost identical symptoms. [68] The difference, broadly speaking, is that depression sometimes, but far from always, is comorbid, that is to say, it is a concomitant symptom in stress reactions. By maintaining the depression perspective, it is possible to sidestep considering the abovementioned work-related stress factors as actually being trauma-inducing – notwithstanding the fact that they are deeply intrusive, undermining and alienating, and that persons subjected to them, in serious cases, risk developing all the symptoms of stress reaction or PTSD. [69]

It is obvious that it is more acceptable to assume that for unspecified reasons, 10-20% of the population in the Western World today – children, adolescents and adults – are suffering from or will come to suffer from depression and in a way that requires medical treatment. And furthermore, it appears more acceptable to surmise that an even greater

---

[67] Andersen, Nielsen & Brinkmann, 2012

[68] See, for instance, ICD-10: a classification system of illnesses and other health-related disorders. This has been drawn up by WHO and used in Europe. DSM-IV is the American diagnosis and classification system for mental disorders. It is also used in Europe for research purposes.

[69] See the discussion in Chapter 5

number of people ought to be treated medically than is the case today. This implies, however, that we are willing to view depression as an aspect of normalcy under the current societal conditions – without bothering to make any further considerations about why this might be the case. Thus, the widespread assumption that depression today is a predictably occurring event in normal people - and that it is depression that makes people unfit for work - contributes to making the whole issue of stress manageable and relatively simple to deal with by our healthcare and therapeutic system.

When we swallow the latter assumption, hook line and sinker, it appears to be almost inconceivable that stress and burnout could be predictable reactions that are unleashed by an unbearable external and inner pressure - predictable reactions which afflict people who are exposed to exploitation and the over-taxation of their human capacities. Or that reifying and alienating control and assessment measures could intimidate, undermine and dehumanize healthy people so they stand in danger of becoming psychically and mentally sick.

Maybe it is high time to take into consideration how the potentials and qualities that human beings actually possess could be used in a much more beneficial way if it is sensible to increase the productivity of their work and performance. Recent results from labor market research demonstrate that corporations that have reintroduced genuine employee participation and are focusing on the performance of core tasks are experiencing a higher level of job satisfaction and increased efficiency as well as a lower rate of sick leave taken. [70]

The work-adjusted concept of competition

It has been said that the first casualty of war is truth. Competition, when it more or less subtly deteriorates into a life-and-death struggle, can be perceived as a precursor to war. If we consider the role that competition plays and how this is expressed in countless ways in our current society, we will probably realize – for instance, in relation to the attaining of market shares or the procurement of contracts and grants – that it is actually a matter of savings one's life at the expense of somebody else's. In such a context of competition, already prior to the outbreak of actual hostilities, there is a risk that truth and trustworthiness come under pressure and are sometimes sacrificed in the service of the cause.

---

70 Limborg, Pedersen, Sørensen, 2008

The newspeak of neoliberal ideology that has been developed within both private-sector and public-sector management has taken the concept of competition to heart, with the result that it has re-emerged with a whole new meaning. "Competition" has become one of our times' most powerful and frequently repeated buzzwords. What has happened is that the original concept of competition – in synch with what has happened to concepts like "value", "flexibility", and "growth" – has been emptied of its content. Subsequently, it has been imbued by new meaning so it fits hand-in-glove with the incessant pursuit of the market to fetch the greatest possible proceeds with as efficient an effort as possible – and preferably in a way that prevents any other players from getting a share of the loot.

Competition is originally, according to its nature – like the urge for and excitement of exploration – related to playing and being joyful. Competition is, in all cultures, known as the thrilling and festive element in which the urge for excitement, joy, and humor breaks the daily life's rhythm of necessary activities and chores. It challenges habitual notions and liberates us to step into the spontaneous and magically open space of the now, in which anything can happen.

A noteworthy example of this could be seen in the TV-documentary: "American Experience: Jesse Owens". [71] *Among other things, the documentary depicts the black athlete's participation in the Olympic Games that were held in Berlin in 1936, during the Nazis' rule of Germany. In one of the four events in which he won, Owens competed against the German athlete, Luz Lang, for the gold medal in the broad jump. This was an event in which Lang, by winning, could demonstrate the superiority of Germany and accordingly the superiority of the Arian race.*

In the qualifying round, Owens twice overstepped the starting mark and was therefore running the risk of being eliminated from the competition if this happened again on his third attempt. Lang took Owens aside and told him to picture a mark an inch or so before the line and to focus on this during his run-up to making the jump. Owens did as he was told and subsequently did not overstep the line again. Henceforth, the two of them competed closely until Owens, in his last jump, surpassed Lang's best jump. At the following ceremony, the gold- and silver-medal winners, respectively, Owens and Lang, could be seen walking around the stadium with their arms linked, smiling, and waving to celebrate the feat. The symbolic significance of Lang's gesture and the joy, shared by the two athletes, of having competed so closely during the entire competition can hardly be overstated

---

71 *American Experience: Jesse Owens.* Directed by Laurens Grant, United States 2012

and stands as exemplary in showing that competition and friendship go hand in hand. [72]

Competition, truth and deceit

The current pressure exerted by the climate of "competition" and hence the fear of being left behind in the race has given rise to the emergence and the increase of completely new forms of untrustworthiness and deceit. The question, however, is whether the dogma of the market society that we have to compete and be the best in order to survive is fundamentally and in itself a deceit – propounded by a minority that is supposedly convinced that competing to achieve as much as possible at the expense of others will paradoxically lead to the best possible conditions in life for everybody in this world. [73]

It may sound a bit exaggerated to juxtapose competition with early stages of war and to emphasize the dubious conditions of veracity in both cases. However, this does not appear at all to be a mistaken association when we reflect on the fact that the financial crisis on Wall Street and the collapse of megabanks in the United States and the rest of the world in the autumn of 2008 are still fresh in our memories. Even if it is hard for us to imagine that it can be true, it has been fully documented that the stock market crashes and the many bank collapses occurred as a logical consequence of deceitful financial transactions, perpetrated by bank managers and their financial advisors – some of whom were professors at the largest and most prestigious universities in the United States. Managers and advisors made staggering multi-million-dollar sums at the detriment of hard-working middle-class Americans who were forced from their homes from one day to the next and, in many cases, also lost their jobs. [74]

---

72 According to historian Tom Ecker, supposedly with Owens as the source, the story about Luz Lang's advice is not true. On the other hand, it is indisputable that the two athletes became good friends and that Owens admired Lang for his courage by so openly showing his friendship with Owens, while Hitler and the Nazi elite were looking on from the grandstands. In Lang's final letter to Owens, before he was killed as a soldier during World War II, he asked Owens to look up his son one day and tell him, "how things can be between men on this Earth" (http://www.npr.org/templates/story/story.php?storyId=111878822)

73 Frank, 2011. Professor of economics Robert Frank convincingly shows that unregulated competition will eventually become counterproductive for both the individual and the common good.

74 Krugman, 2012. According to the American economist and Nobel Prize laureate, Paul Krugman, there is a long tradition for abundant flows of money to bosses within high finance. In 2006, the 25 highest paid hedge-fund managers in the United States, for instance, made 14 billion dollars which, between them, amounts to three times the total salaries of all the 80,000 teachers in New York City.

When the banks were subsequently bailed out – a bailout that was paid for by the very same Americans' tax dollars – the same deceitful managers and their advisors were the first to receive hundreds of millions of dollars in severance pay, on top of the gigantic sums they had scored from American homeowners, in the wake of the collapse. Incidentally, many of the advisors returned to their positions as professors of economics at their respective universities and still they, through their private consultancy businesses, continue to serve as top advisors in the financial world as well as in important advisory institutions. [75]

We can only wonder at the fact that at the same time that these deceits were devastating the means of existence of millions of Americans and other people around the world, billions of dollars were being spent to "fight terror" abroad and at home. The regulation and the constant monitoring of ordinary peoples' lives and activities has come to be firmly established, while at the same time governments all over the world have been reluctant to find ways of controlling the destabilization of financial capital.

The unchallenged dogma about the necessity of competition in order to acquire an ever-increasing profit and secure survival at the expense of others is a distorted and cynical perception of reality. It is deceitful in that it has been able to overshadow the unique ability and natural urge of human beings to cooperate, and also to overshadow that this ability and this urge have been, under widely different conditions of life, preconditions for the very survival of the human species.

Perhaps it is high time to remember how lies and deceit have been the main ingredients in the takeovers of totalitarian regimes and how new despots have been able to keep people in the clutches of a distorted reality with the use of inhuman force. Under such conditions, corrupting people all the way down to the bottom of the hierarchy has been an easy task, eliciting the concomitant effects that citizens, for one thing, develop a deep mistrust of others and, secondly, have their sense of reliability undermined.

The normalization of untruthfulness

Most people living in our democratic society would claim that untruthfulness and deceit are evils that we, in any event, must prevent. Similarly, we are willing, if worst comes to worst, to offer our lives for the sake

---

[75] E.g., Noam Chomsky has criticized the Obama administration and its choice of economic top advisors, http://www.zcommunications.org/chomsky-sessions-3-education-and-economics-part-i-by-noam-chomsky.html

of the truth and that which is dear to us. Truthfulness and trustworthiness seem to be indestructible ethical values that we will safeguard at all times.

If we take a more personal angle in our approach to this issue, we can also observe that there are many who would assert that being subjected to untruthfulness and deceit is repugnant and deeply harmful. Similarly, most people, if they had subjected others to untruthfulness and deceit, would have a very hard time. Any suggestion that truthfulness and trustworthiness are under pressure in our own democratic market society and any suggestion that this situation is fomenting a risk of corrupting people, from the top to the bottom, will very likely be snubbed and be refuted with protestations about our civilized stage of development and about the fundamental values of our democracy.

If we, for a moment, leave aside abstract notions about our appreciation of truth and take a direct view our immediate reality, we will be able to observe a somewhat more varied everyday handling of truth. In fact, it would not be all that outlandish to admit that we are, in fact, lying from time to time and that we are sometimes obtaining extra profits by shortchanging the customer. However, as is often pointed out, this is the normal state of affairs - and it has always been this way. It is actually considered a matter of course that human beings have a tendency to succumb to the temptation to deceive others by embellishing reality a little in order to stay out of trouble or to achieve something that is considered impossible to obtain in an honest way.

There has to be some truth in humanity's contentious relationship to truthfulness. Thus, when we turn to the world religions, it is noteworthy that they have lain down explicit commands stating that we are not allowed to lie. Such commands seem to bear witness to the fact that it is a widespread fallibility dwelling in us and that lying is considered so repugnant and undermining that we have to lay down commands against doing it.

Today, when it comes to safeguarding to the truth, we have judicial statutes to guide us but no longer written laws and commands that were issued by some ultimate authority that we have to obey. Nevertheless, it becomes impressed on us early in our lives that we are not allowed to lie. Most parents are actually a bit surprised when their small child, who can hardly speak, says, for the first time, something that is not true – often with an expression on its face that discloses that the child is trying out lying, as a possibility. It is thus often, when a child gets caught in the act for the first time, that the child gets chided and receives an admonishment counseling him/her not to lie anymore. This is not to say that this might be an innate trait that will, sooner or later, manifest itself in the development process of the child. On the contrary, it is quite likely that we are dealing with behavior that is acquired through imitation. Even very small children have extraordinarily good opportunities to learn lying in multifarious ways from their immediate surroundings, for instance, when their parents employ the shortcut of untruthfulness to have *their* way in relation to the child.

It might seem that we know and that we feel, deep down, that not being truthful is reproachable while, at the same time, we are more than happy when we are not taking this too seriously and are not being all too moralizing about being untruthful. In this way, our honesty about evading the truth makes lying appear ordinary, harmless, and everyday.

The questions, however, are whether it is possible to normalize untruthfulness and whether we are willing – for instance, if we believe that it might benefit us or might benefit the common good – to allow lying in certain situations ... and in measured doses. And whether we, in the long run, are able put up with this. In the following sections, these questions will be elucidated through the means of concrete examples.

Prescribed untrustworthiness
In my capacity as a supervisor of psychologists, I have been faced, time and time again, with employees from both public-sector jobs and private enterprises who have been instructed to slacken the quality of their work, in order to circumvent laws and contracts by which their jobs are covered, as well as to lie about aspects of what they are doing. However, what happens to employees when leaders at their workplace instruct them to be untrustworthy in carrying out their work? What happens when they are prevented from being in tune with their professional expertise, their fundamental values and their ethical attitudes? The following concrete – and for many employees in both public-sector jobs and private enterprises, the following recognizable – example manifested itself in a supervision session that I administered to psychologists who were employed by a municipal institution:

A case on untrustworthiness

These neuropsychologists had been instructed, in connection with yet another cost-cutting exercise and with the upgrading of computerized organization and management programs, to enhance the efficiency of their work. This entailed that they henceforth had to carry out examinations and the treatment of brain-damaged patients using a reduced number of hours that did not allow sufficient time for making an appropriate professional examination. Moreover, with this reduced quantity of hours, administering treatment was utterly out the question.

The neuropsychologists were furthermore assigned the additional task of keeping tabs on and reporting the time consumption of the various daily work functions – for instance, different forms of patient contact, written reports and evaluations, email and telephone contact with other involved professionals, daily professional supervision, counseling, and spontaneously arising conversations during the day that had to do with case files and so forth. On the basis of this quality assurance procedure, computations related to the quality of their work performance and productivity were allegedly carried out.

I knew the neuropsychologists from a lengthy course of supervision in which we had gradually spent more and more time dealing with their working conditions and the very negative influences that these had on their abilities to carry out their jobs. Valuable supervision time that was originally supposed to be used for case supervision was used instead on figuring out ways in which the neuropsychologists could steer clear of the increasingly absurd working conditions.

At the start of the supervision session, they concurrently expressed confusion, despair, and powerlessness and they were experiencing a considerable degree of professional and personal insecurity. Clearly shocked, they told me how they, as they once again approached the manager – who was not a psychologist – had tried to make it clear that they were no longer able, taking the new time frames into consideration, to perform their jobs in a professionally qualified and meaningful way. Even before they had finished, they were met with undisguised attacks on their efforts and were given plain orders – and even threats – to "fall in line".

The criticism voiced by their manager was that they were too empathic – in the sense of being too softhearted – toward the brain damaged patients and that they had gotten too carried away with performing their jobs professionally. They had to forget about matters of "professional quality" until they were "off the clock" again because the bottom-line problem was simply that they were not making enough money for the institution.

To my feignedly astounded question asking them rhetorically whether we, as municipally employed psychologists, were put in the world to make money, I was instructed that it actually was preferable if you were a "cash cow". This meant that you, like other employees, were supposed to perform your job in seven hours instead of in the ten hours that had been approved by the referring institutions. When you were able to comply with this requirement, the payment for those remaining three hours would nonetheless be paid out to one's own workplace. Hence, the workplace would be able to take on more contracts from referring and paying municipalities. And this would contribute, in turn, to ensuring that the institution, also in the future, would be receiving the necessary public grants.

The psychologists mentioned in the example were, in other words, being told to change their assessment of what is professionally and ethically proper and of what makes sense in their work. Under the threat of being fired for being "unprofitable" to their workplace, their professional and personal integrity were being demeaned and devalued.

Regardless of the job functions they were involved in, they had to be ever vigilant with themselves and make sure that they were performing the job correctly, as gauged by standards that were obscure to them and that were based on insufficient knowledge about the job that was accordingly being monitored and assessed. Eventually, the control of the psychologists and their self-reporting took up so much of their time and concentration at the job that this aspect of their daily activity appeared to be more important than the professional psychological work they were actually supposed to perform.

What was most unbearable for them, however, was that they had to sit face to face, on a daily basis, with sick people and be dishonest and underhanded.

The reaction of the psychologists was a predictable combination of powerlessness and grief that the job they were qualified for and which they knew could bring about considerable improvement in their patients' ability to function could simply not be performed at their workplace. They were – like most employees in analogous situations – clearly marked by having lost their confidence in whether they really were good enough for their jobs. The psychologists, having worked as neuropsychologists for, respectively, four and ten years, expressed grave doubts about whether they could trust their own judgment and their own professional capability at all.

One factor contributing to their sense of doubt about themselves was their perception that their colleagues from other fields were apparently able to manage. So, this being the case, *there had to be something wrong with them.*

When untrustworthiness hits home

The above is just one of many examples of employees being ordered to circumvent laws and contracts and perform jobs that they cannot conscientiously support. They are being asked, furthermore, to cover over deceitful behavior, out of their loyalty to their workplace and motivated by their fear of losing their jobs. We might have become used to hearing stories about, for instance, IT experts who not only have to put in absurdly long working hours but also have to accept that the products they deliver are not ready to be used and faulty because there is no way that the contractual obligations can be fulfilled. They will subsequently be held responsible, anyway, regardless of the fact that management has knowingly entered into an underfunded contract. However, the fact that this also happens in public-sector workplaces can be hard to fathom and difficult to come to terms with. [76]

As a supervisor working in the service of municipalities, I have witnessed many variations on this theme. This could involve, for instance, cases of recommendation related to the compulsory removal of children in families tainted by incest and neglect. The exercise has been to drag things out in time, officially with a view to finding other solutions, regardless of the fact that everybody knows that the real reason is that the city, for financial reasons, has decreed a freeze on all high-cost measures during the present fiscal year. In many cases, out-of-home placements are being denied by the city's social committee with recourse taken in the claim that these children need to keep their connection with their parents, notwithstanding the fact that the parents might be inflicting deep and lasting injuries on them.

---

76 A similar example of forced dishonesty was cited in an article in the Danish Psychological Association's magazine with the title "Crushed under the bottom line", see Ahrensbach et al., 2012. The writers of this article are all psychologists and union representatives in the psychiatry department of the Copenhagen regional health authority

When, after a while, charges are inevitably pressed against the parents of the neglected and abused children and when the cases enter the public eye, these caseworkers will find themselves denounced in the national media for their sloppiness in handling the casework, and for their lack of professional competence. This happens at the very same time that administrative managers and social committee chairmen, for instance, are swearing on the television news broadcasts that all the rules have been followed, to the letter, and that there is nothing, on this count, to latch onto.

It is important to realize that caseworkers are standing in imminent danger of being subjected to *secondary traumatization* when they know about the terrible conditions in families in which children are being grossly neglected and abused. This is something we can easily ascertain when we consider our own reactions to unbearable stories and to the images of these, when they are covered in newspapers and as they are shown on TV.

But there is, furthermore, a case of the *primary traumatization* of caseworkers when they are not respected for their professional competencies and their proficiency during casework. The lack of ongoing endorsement by their managers becomes contributory to primary traumatization because the caseworkers are bereft of any support and are deprived of any real opportunity to take responsibility for performing a qualified job with at-risk families. As a consequence, their recommendations for appropriate concrete measures are running the risk of being denied and they may even have to suffer the disgrace of being pilloried publicly.

Being a supervisor, what I – and a growing number of other specialists, as well – have witnessed is that managers and employees who are working in educational, healthcare and social institutions are developing work-related traumatic stress syndrome. An increasing number of these individuals will, in addition, permanently lose their ability to work. With this evidence at hand, there can be no doubt that the uppermost management of workplaces has turned against their own and that the employees are being subjected to abuse.

> *The recently deceased German writer, Christa Wolf, was a citizen of communist East Germany. All her life, she supported a socialist society. Already during the Cold War, however, she openly criticized the leadership. In the period 1959-61, she was an informant for Stasi but, due to her failure to submit reports, Stasi lost interest in her as a*

collaborator, and she became [77] a prominent dissident, and was subsequently monitored closely for the next 30 years. In her latest book, Christa Wolf describes how people of good will are driven into a fix, in which they cannot do what is right on the basis of their own moral compass. When that happens, she claims, their society is fatally ill.

The question is whether we are willing to admit that in a society that develops symptoms of fatal illness, we, as citizens, are already threatened by annihilation ourselves.

When reality has to be redefined in order to be endured

It is basically known by everybody who is cognizant of double-binding situations' damaging consequences that it is impossible to learn how to be – or to become better at being – in a double-binding situation. Being in a double-bind means that no matter whatever one does it will *always* be wrong, either in relation to oneself or others, or both. Double-binding situations are considered deeply destructive to our physical and emotional wellbeing.

Even though it might not be possible to avoid a double-binding situation, it is necessary to redefine it. One way of doing this is to reinterpret one's own perception of self and the world so that it matches the externally determined interpretation of reality. This is similar to the adjustment behavior exhibited by hostages who develop "the Stockholm syndrome". In order to endure unbearable life-threatening situations, the hostage constructs a split perception of reality. Inasmuch as the hostage submits and enters into an unholy alliance with the hostage-taker, the hostage vacillates between perceiving the hostage-taker as life-threatening, on the one hand, while perceiving, on the other hand, oneself and the hostage-taker as each other's saviors in relation to a threatening world. [78]

In order for the employee to succeed in attuning his or her interpretation of reality – in order for this interpretation to become labor-market relevant – the person in question has to suppress or dissociate him/herself from the discomfort, the indignation and the pain of compromising with his/her own basic professional and ethical values, thus alienating the employee from him- or herself. This is a survival strategy that is harmful in the long run and which does not alleviate the resulting state of high stress. Instead, it is encapsulating it in a latent chronic high stress condition. This may manifest itself by apparently inexplicable physical

---

77) Wolf, C. (2014): City of Angels or The Overcoat of Dr. Freud, Farrar, Strauss and Giroux, New York
78 The same defense mechanism is also developed in children from highly dysfunctional families

discomfort: for instance, states of pain, heart-rhythm problems, or actual physical disease, as well as emotional imbalances, including anxiety and depression.

Conformist individualism

Just like Christa Wolf, Hannah Arendt warned that people, in their eagerness to be of use, act automatically to live up to the prevailing norms of the time. [79] During the totalitarian societies of the 20th century, this proved to have catastrophic consequences. What has failed to receive much attention, however, is that a similar attitude and submissive behavior – under the influence of subtler jet deeply invasive measures in a democratic society – are bringing about serious psychic and physical effects. This is the case when a person, in an effort to adapt – in order to avoid becoming a burden to his/her colleagues at the workplace and avoid being marginalized and ostracized – chooses to "go with the flow" and fit in.

All the aforementioned work-related stress factors contain an element of intimidation and alienation. This is the case whether we are dealing with the simplest of them - the overburdening of the individual with a back-breaking workload - or whether the control- and assessment-systems are inflicting the deconstruction of authentic sense of identity and self-esteem: a deconstruction that makes room for the reified view of humanity of modern management. Subsequently, this forms the "foundation" for the construction of an externally and situationally determined perception of oneself and of the world. In its fully evolved manifestation, what we are dealing with here is a personality construction that could be coined "conformist individualism". The point of departure for this personality construction is that there is a primary focus on the identity of the individual as he/she is functioning as a citizen and as an employee and that the person only to a lesser degree is regarded as a human being, in his or her own right.

The view of humanity and society that is supported by modern management influences development and learning, and radically so. From nursery school to the education system encountered in one's adult life, the path is paved so as to fulfill a certain purpose, which rests on a specific value-based make-up of society. This, however, occurs in the guise of the educational system's individual teaching plans, which are

---
79 Arendt, 1958. Arendt considers the individual isolation and loneliness of the citizens as preconditions of their totalitarian subjugation

presumably adapted to the individual student. In a corresponding way, employees will continuously be assigned courses that supposedly have the purpose of upgrading the individual's personal and professional competences.

The resulting individualization and the emphasis on the individual's responsibility and freedom to shape his or her own development and learning will, under these conditions, be rather illusory and could be perceived as a manipulation of concepts and people. The individual who opens up to standardization, manipulation and control may develop a personal and professional profile that is consistent with societal needs. At the same time, systems of evaluation and sanction may suppress personal qualities and attitudes that are either considered irrelevant or seem to be in conflict with the prevailing societal needs.

The conformist individualist thereby runs the risk of developing a failing ability when it comes to thinking independently, being reflecting, and self-reflecting based on empathy, having self-insight and taking care of oneself. At the same time, the conformist individualist may, to a still higher degree, be left to pursue an incessant, unfulfilled and self-absorbed quest for a fitting identity and for being able to *feel* him/herself. Meaning and fulfillment of life may increasingly be based on prevailing opinions and standards that promise prestige. Because the person's own inner guidance has been ordered underground, so to speak, the person risks being left to relating to his or her life, and to his/her own qualities and competencies, by measuring and comparing him/herself with others, on the basis of ever-changing notions of what it is to be successful and do well.

The deficient empathic contact, which characterizes the conformist individualist in relation to him/herself, also subsumes his/her relationship to others. This is a possible explanation for why the conformist individualist increasingly perceives reality on the level of ideas and, to an ever-increasing extent, takes his/her inspiration from simplistic messages that easily float around as time-based opinions making up the collective understanding of reality. An understanding of reality that has been created and legitimized by convenient opinions, which imperceptibly become prejudices that might sometimes be directed at the multitude of individuals who, for very different reasons, find themselves in the category of citizens that are being marginalized at a given time. This could include people on sick leave, the unemployed or uneducated, the poor, and foreigner. In other words, the category of citizens from which the conformist individualist is trying very hard to distance him- or herself.

Research with the telescope to the blind eye

The solution to the dilemma faced by psychologists, teachers, nurses, doctors and caseworkers is not to be found in the practice of saying, "Never mind", as is so earnestly recommended by managers and leading stress experts. Nor is the solution to be found, to put it a different way, in having people to unlearn their "perfectionism" and "over-involvement" and become more adept at disregarding the quality of their work. Such recommendations do not take into account that a stress reaction can be the human answer to an inhumane situation and that the greatest "problem" experienced by people who are seriously affected by stress, in many cases, is that they cannot bear to work contrary to fundamental human values that make sense and that are indisputable to them.

Stress research that adopts the perspective of examining who it is that succumbs to stress and what personality factors of the individual are the causes of not being able to "cut it" in the current labor market runs the risk of giving legitimacy to job-related dehumanizing. Moreover, stress coaching, various forms of therapy, and mindfulness meditation run the same risk when these methods are used with the intention of making an individual capable of enduring dehumanizing working conditions.

The question is whether it is all that meritorious to be trained to successfully endure dehumanization's devastation of unique human qualities while at the same time we can see how colleagues, family members and friends, for whom this is not an option are suffering from work-related psychic disorders for which they are receiving medical treatment.

At times, it is tempting to ask whether social scientists, anthropologists, philosophers, stress researchers, and psychotherapists have a tendency to put the telescope to the blind eye, thus taking up a position from which opinions are formed about current affairs and about what is to be done in response to the pressing challenges of the times. Do we, for instance, know how students, employees, and managers generally experience reification and externally determined alienation? Have we ourselves been exposed to this?

The answer to the latter question is, inevitably: "Of course we have!" – Which also answers the former question. Even free and independent spirits are influenced by society and the conditions that we, as active participants, live in and contribute to shaping. Philosophers, scientists and psychotherapists are also subjected to the same conditions as the people we theorize about, conduct studies of, and treat, whether we admit this or not. The relevant questions we might ask ourselves are, then: how do we choose to approach this; and how does each and every one of us come to terms with the fact that we are also afflicted? For it is highly unlikely that we, as researchers and psychotherapists, should be counted among the few exceptions that are perched high above the commotion and the unrelenting reality of the world.

The widespread tendency that scientists – who, like everyone else, are subjected to continual control and contract management – rush research projects and articles through in order to perform and show results provides clear evidence of this. Research thereby runs the risk of tilting its perspective from acquiring new and relevant knowledge to being an end in itself. This is apparent when a researcher – working under the pressure of meeting the deadlines delineated by the terms of contract management – is forced to present results for the purpose of gaining access to further funding, in cutthroat competition with other researchers. Research thereby risks taking on a life of its own and being ruled by its own laws – emptied of substance and meaning and conducted by researchers who cannot bear to acknowledge that their research is a mirror in which they see themselves and their inner feelings of meaninglessness, impotence and self-deception.

When scientific status is bestowed on urban legends

Many urban legends about stress and treatment of stress are circulating. In recent years, they seem, by virtue of a kind of repetition-compulsion, to have acquired the status of scientifically supported knowledge and they have gained currency in social-scientific articles and books and public debates. This is, for instance, the case with the repeated statements that people afflicted by work-related stress are too perfectionist and too over-involved, that they are unusually vulnerable as an outgrowth of previous trauma, or that they have domestic problems. Or that people become sick by being on sick leave – period! The argument that sick leave therefore has to avoided suffers from the same logical flaws as when a seriously ill person who requires treatment is advised not to go into the hospital because the mortality rate is higher inside the hospital than in the surrounding society.

It is indisputable that a person who is on sick leave and requires rehabilitation-treatment and who does not receive rehabilitation-treatment during the sick leave is running a risk of getting even sicker during the leave. [80] Thus, a person who goes on sick leave due to work-related stress

---

80 Høgelund, 2012. It is rendered probable that in cases of specific illnesses – for instance, with back problems and other cases of decreased functionality in the motor apparatus – faster recovery has been reported when people on sick leave have been able to do their jobs, with a reduction in work hours and under special considerations of care, while the person is being treated.

and who is not taking part in a relevant rehabilitation program will have only modest chances of recovery from the stress reaction and is, furthermore, running the risk of developing depression.

If, however, the same person is immediately offered qualified treatment, the person will have optimum chances to recover after he or she gets the time necessary to get well without interference and pressure from the outside world. Furthermore, there will be very few cases where medical treatment for depression are needed and similarly, there will be a far better chance of avoiding relapses after the person has resumed work. [81]

Another urban legend clamors for being exorcised: Human beings do not develop sociophobia when they succumb to stress. On the contrary, the person tends to pay attention to the signals broadcast by the organism that protection is needed because the nervous system is in a state of chronic high stress. In this condition, the person experiences hypersensitivity toward what is experienced as unbearable overstimulation, both externally and internally. In order to obey the needs of the organism the person must, for a certain period of time, opt out of social contact and disclaim responsibility for living up to the pressures and expectations associated with functioning normally. In this way, the system avoids becoming inundated by impulses, thoughts and feelings that the individual is simply unable to handle.

One of the first signs that a person is in the process of a successful rehabilitation is that tendencies toward unhappiness and depression subside and that the urge for isolation is diminished and disappears altogether during the course of the rehabilitation period.

Emancipation from the hegemony of dehumanization and alienation

Behind the distorted mask of conformist individualism, we hold everything that it takes to turn the tide and bring an end to the devastating alienation from our precious human qualities. The alternative to the consistent undermining of people in the name of competition must be to make room for cooperation in an atmosphere of mutual trust, honesty and respect.

Imagining that we can possibly survive if we continue to let ourselves be guided by deeply narcissistic and grandiose ideas of having to become the best in the world is nothing other than a grand illusion. Con-

---

81 Praetorius (2007)

sidering the previous century's devastating consequences, where people were seduced, time and again, by uncontrollable urges to seize dominion of the world, it is alarming that we seem to still be singing variations of the same tune.

The question is whether it is even possible to reclaim the land that has been lost within ourselves and emancipate ourselves from the hegemony of reification and alienation. The treatments administered to trauma victims like hostages, prisoners of war and others who have been subjected to abuse, repression, and dehumanization offer testimony that we can indeed lose contact with the free and unfettered access to ourselves and our qualities. That we, for some period of time, can lose track of what makes sense to us on a deep level. However, in my own practice working with stress-rehabilitation and in the extensive exploration of and historiography related to humanity's many thousands of years on Earth, we can find evidence that it is not possible to permanently destroy the indestructible qualities and potentials that make us the human beings we are.

The exposure of and the clash with reification and dehumanization are conducted with our being willing to open our eyes and see the distorted reality that we find ourselves in. Not a reality that exists outside us and relates only to others but a reality that we are subject to and of which we are co-creators, until such time as we decide to liberate ourselves. It requires a persistent, honest and conscious effort to establish, develop and maintain a trusting and authentic contact with ourselves and with our potentials and qualities, and this requires that we, in spite of everything, find the courage to express these potentials and qualities openly, in communion with others.

PART II
EXPLORING THE HUMAN POTENTIAL

CHAPTER 5
DEVELOPMENT: EMPATHIC COOPERATION OR ALIENATING SUBMISSION?

The point of departure taken in this chapter is a field study that I carried out on a small Polynesian Island. The findings from my study showed - perhaps not surprisingly - that socialization in childhood and attitudes to child rearing was conditioned by the living conditions and the history and culture of the people. The surprising outcome from my stay on the island, however, was that I came to realize deeply problematic issues around socialization in our own society. Factors that play a crucial role also for learning and maturing processes in the educational system and in the workplace later in life.

From this point of departure, it is shown, that the market society's ideal of the socioeconomically relevant human being and the growing application of control and evaluation methods for purposes of aligning the development, the learning, and the maturation processes of the citizens constitute the foundation of inner estrangement and alienation. It leaves both the child and subsequently the adult in a situation where he or she, due to his/her dependency on the authorities, is forced to enter into contracts in order to gain acceptance and avoid expulsion.

The chapter also presents groundbreaking scientific studies of the early mother-child relationship and a theory of the maturation process in the context of an authentic and healthy personality formation. The obvious social relevance of today's extensive knowledge of the development and maturation processes are outlined.

The wonder of the unpredictable

Occasionally, when I feel overwhelmed by the enormous overflow of knowledge, complexity and paradoxes in our global information society, I return, in my imagination, to Mungiki, a small Polynesian island in the South Pacific Ocean. Mungiki is not an island concocted by my fantasy like the ones that we, in our daydreams, are tempted to escape to, in order to find some peace and quiet and just relax. No, Mungiki is a very real island that I stayed at many years ago, while undertaking a cross-cultural field study.

The purpose of my "travelling back" to Mungiki is to "get back to basics" and see things more simply and straightforwardly. When I feel challenged by what I – and the whole world, for that matter – are being confronted with right now, I ask myself: "How would *that* appear from the perspective of life on Mungiki?" Or in other words – as life appears in its most pragmatic simplicity.

The point of departure of my field study in Mungiki was to investigate the socialization of aggression and aggressive behavior. The purpose was to get to know and to understand the adult Mungikis' behavior toward each other and hence make a documentation of another unique and indigenous people.

As a researcher investigating "real life" out there in the field, you are quite often confronted by something unpredictable, which you didn't have any clue about whatsoever while planning the project for the investigation. This is a common experience that is shared by researchers doing field studies. Researchers who stay for extended stretches of time in a culture other than their own generally experience yet another feature in common: they, almost unanimously, express how much they, in studying a foreign culture, learn about themselves and their own culture. Realizing how much I still had to learn about myself and my own culture – as viewed from the perspective and way of life of the Mungikis – I returned home from my stay on Mungiki.

I still draw on this realization. The following account demonstrates this.

Perspectives on childrearing in a Polynesian Island

> *It was not until several months after making a field study I had conducted on the Polynesian island of Mungiki (Bellona) that I came, during the task of going through the data gathered from my interviews, to understand what was truly interesting about my study.* [82] *It was not the information that was provided by the answers to those questions but rather the insight that arose in connection with my subsequent reflections on the data and on my experience of the life lived on the island.*

82　Praetorius, 1970

The Mungikis, an indigenous people, live on a tiny coral island in the Pacific and have only sparse contact with the outside world. The island, which is six miles long and three miles wide, is divided into three districts. These have – according to the Mungikis' approximately 300-year long history – had ongoing conflicts about the delineation of borders and ownership of the land. Especially earlier on, these conflicts escalated into violence, resulting in killing and maiming. Even though peace agreements have, over the years, been settled and even though there have been intermittent attempts to determine the ownership of the land, old grudges can occasionally flare up and conflicts sometimes erupt, leading once again to violence.

The Mungikis are not very proud of this aspect of their history. On the contrary, they are ashamed of it and they still blame themselves today for getting so carried away by resentment and anger at the thought of having been put at a disadvantage. They are also very wary of talking about this, out of fear that merely speaking about it may trigger new open conflicts.

The Danish cross-cultural researcher professor, Dr. Torben Monberg, had – after several prolonged stays on the island – developed a thorough knowledge of the Mungikis, their culture and their history. During his stays on the island he had observed that the Mungikis made use of corporal punishment of their children from the time of their infancy. [83] *He therefore suggested that I undertake an investigation of the process of socialization in order to uncover circumstances that could be said to cause the development of violent conflict behavior in adult Mungikis and to examine whether they could be considered an especially aggressive people.* [84]

I had not been staying on the island for very long before I got confirmation about the Mungikis' corporal methods of disciplining their children. In Denmark, slapping a child would be considered a severe form of abuse and is prohibited by law. I have to confess that I inwardly disapproved of the corporal punishment in Mungiki and considered the slapping as signifying a lack of empathy toward the little children.

---

83 Monberg, 1966
84 Mead, 1956. At the time, cross-cultural psychology was inspired by, e.g., Margaret Mead's comparative anthropological studies of "primitive" societies.

My long list of questions regarding the motives for and the use of disciplining methods included a number of questions that dealt with what in my own society are altogether legal and frequently used forms of child-rearing, such as threatening the child with, or actually resorting to (albeit temporary), exclusion from the community – for example, by saying, "If you do not behave yourself when we are eating together, you cannot take part and you will have to leave". I furthermore inquired into ways of disciplining methods for setting up conditions and asked about their manner of uttering verbal statements that might signal disapproval of the child. I also asked whether the granting of goods was conditioned upon the child's behavior and conduct, for instance: "If you behave yourself, if you are nice, etc., you will obtain this and that..."

It took quite a long time for the Mungikis to even understand these questions. The questions had to be rephrased several times and related to hypothetical situations in their everyday lives. When, at last, they realized what this child-rearing method revolves around, they were appalled! In their eyes, these ways of disciplining children were downright cruel and using them would be completely out of the question. Spontaneously, they added that even if their children could be unruly, they nonetheless loved them.

The frank corporal punishment was a reaction to the actual behavior – not a rejection of the child.

To my question: "At what age do you stop slapping the children?" the prompt answer was: "When they run faster than their parents."

The field study was conducted in keeping with anthropological studies of "primitive" societies and complied with every standard procedure that is generic to scientific research, a standard procedure that is maintained to this very day. [85] Originally, my field study was targeted at confirming the hypothesis that the Mungikis are a particularly aggressive people, when correlated with studies of other peoples and societies, including our own. Had I confined my research strictly within the scope charted out by the study's point of departure and had I focused narrow-mindedly on the questions and answers spun from the chosen examination method, it is quite likely that I would have concluded that the Mungikis are, in fact, a particularly aggressive people, basing this conclusion on, among other things, their widespread use of corporal punishment in the process of socialization.

---

85 Whiting et al., 1966 and Kaplan, 1961 could be mentioned here

There were, however, several reasons why I could not arrive at such a convenient and simple conclusion. First of all, the conditions of life, the make-up of the society, and the social norms were so fundamentally different that it did not make sense to attempt to conduct a comparative study. Second, such a conclusion was simply not consistent with my general impression of life on the island. To me, the Mungikis seemed to be empathic, generous, and kind-hearted, and they seemed to be doing well together in their daily activities. Their conditions of life implied that they were all deeply dependent on each other and their living conditions, and they cooperated with each other and shared crops and catches from the ocean, knowing quite well that this was a question of their very survival. As if it were the most natural thing to do, the Mungikis were genuinely and intensely interested in me, and they were open and considerate toward me, right from the day that I was brought, in a canoe, safely from the ship to the shore of the island and up until they, some months later, waved goodbye to me.

My field study's most important contribution to insight and knowledge sprang from my subsequent reflections on my own society's use of psychological disciplining methods administered toward children – methods that potentially threaten the involved parties and also serve to signal that the child's attachment to the community is conditioned by the way the child perform and behaves.

Perhaps it could be objected that the effects of this child-rearing practice should not be exaggerated, as it is not that common and that it must be considered relatively harmless. But if we stop and consider the prevalence of this practice and its basic mindset, as it has increasingly come to be displayed in the widespread administration of management, control, evaluation and assessment methods – within both the educational sector and the labor market – a somewhat different picture emerges. This is something that we can assure ourselves by observing how children, adolescents and adults are subjected to harmonization, adjustment of opinions, and behavior regulation under the more or less subtle threats of marginalization and exclusion. In reality, this constitutes a threat to and a deflation of the person. That this practice is far from harmless will be further elucidated later in this chapter, where we will be examining some of the concrete consequences for the individual's perception of self and the world.

Like most other scientific studies based on qualitative methods, my field study invites the following observations:

1. *It is not necessarily the answers to the questions we ask that are significant but rather the insight and the knowledge that may emerge in situations wherein we exchange questions and answers, as well as when we subsequently reflect upon the communication.*

2. *That the surprising value of research results appears in the form of unanticipated insights, while the research method turns out to be problematic.*

3. *That a research situation can contribute to renewed reflections on the perception of human beings and of society, where the researcher is not limited to slavishly following the laid-down research strategy during the processing of data. This freedom of inquiry makes room for discovering and wondering about the unforeseen and for ascribing meaning to it.*

Blind spots and eye openers

Both when we are doing research and when we are making room, in our daily lives, for reflecting upon our conventional attitudes and our ways of being in the world, we will inevitably be confronted from time to time by our own blind spots that effectively paper over the fact that we, unthinkingly, actually legitimize and practice attitudes and behavior that are fundamentally uncaring and unethical.

The study of cultures other than our own can function as an incomparable eye opener. The realization that respective differences, in principle, can serve as a source of insight and provide us with new knowledge, not just about the other culture but also about ourselves, can, from this point of view, be as important and rewarding as all the comparisons we are so very prone to making.

One thing that has caught my attention, not only on Mungiki but also in other non-Western cultures where I have had the opportunity to visit and reside, is that children, from the time of their infancy and long after they have learned to walk, are in close physical contact with the mother or other close caregivers. Children are carried around and take part in everyday activities with the mother and other family members, just as they sleep with their parents and other siblings – often in one large sleeping place intended for the entire family.

As we have become more prosperous and as our homes have become larger, it has increasingly come to be taken for granted in our societies that every child has his or her own room and that children, already at an early age, should be taught to sleep in their own beds. At the same time, they are being separated, quite early on – that is, before they can take care of themselves – from the mother and from the rest of the family as they start to attend day-care because the developments in society dictate that both parents work away from the home.

In the animal kingdom, this separation from the caregiver does not take place until after the young progenies can take care of themselves. Researchers who observe animals in their natural habitat have stated that humanity, whose offspring take the longest time to become independent, is also the species that, curiously enough, displays the slightest natural faculty for providing closeness and care to their still dependent children. [86] [87]

It appears that we, in our societies, are not aware of the most basic need of small children for the secure base in close physical and emotional contact with the mother or other important and consistent caregivers. In reality, though, we do know quite a lot and are much more aware of this today, owing to the past 40-50 years of intense studies centered on child development and conditions of maturation.

Groundbreaking research on the human processes of formation

The youth revolution with the concomitant hippie movement at the end of the 1960s was, in part, an expression of the wish to break away from the authoritarian organization of society and its institutions. The young people's opposition against the authoritarian attitude was also articulated in suggested modifications of the relation between adults and children and in the position of children in society. The wish to ex-

---

[86] Byrnit, 2007
[87] Tsoknyi Rinpoche, 2012. In this context, the fact that Tibetan Buddhist teachers, who have been teaching Buddhist philosophy and practice to students from the West for around the past 40 years, were rather uncomprehending at first when their students would express a lack of self-confidence and low self-esteem gives food for thought. And they were also rather uncomprehending that many of the aspiring students stated having a strained relationship with their parents, whom they felt had not been sufficiently supportive during their childhood. Eventually, there seems to be a widespread understanding – especially among some of the younger teachers, with a sound knowledge of Western culture and language – that students from the West need to heal fragile parts of their own personality formation before it is advisable to work with the more complex areas of Buddhist theory and engage in the meditation practices.

plore alternative types of social life arose out of a recognition that children and parents have a basic need to give and receive closeness and care in an environment with flexible possibilities of development for children and adults. It is these very needs that had been neglected during the formation of the industrialized and technological market society.

In the same years, results from the groundbreaking scientific exploration of the mother-child relation as well as observations and experiments performed with animals gradually became known and gained recognition among a wider public. The new departure – which was pitted against the conventional and dominant mindset and practice within scientific research – was based, first of all, on the researchers' wish to explore what actually takes place in the early mother-child relation and to explore what it is that stimulates the child's coming-into-the-world as a unique person.

The process of unearthing the significance of early socialization for a secure, supportive and healthy process of development was initiated by scientists within psychology and medicine. In the time leading up to and after World War II, these researchers highlighted the significance of the mother-child relationship or the relationship between the child and a continuous and stable caregiver in the child's first years. Subsequently, research has been conducted that inquire into the conditions under which a healthy process of development can be continued later in childhood as well as in the process of the maturation of potentials and qualities in adulthood.

The significance of the mother-child relationship for the child's healthy development became a center of attention as a result of research findings in the 1930s that shed light on the dire consequences of separating the mother from her child during hospitalization and institutionalization. This problem was actualized once again during World War II, in situations where children were separated from their mothers, either as a consequence of protecting the children from the harm of the war or because the mother – and frequently because both parents – had been deported or killed.

René Spitz was one of the first researchers with a background within psychology and medicine to conduct observations of, on the one hand, children suffering from severe developmental disorders after long-term hospitalization or institutionalization and, on the other, normally developed children who had not experienced such separation. [88]

---
88 Spitz, 1945

The research that Spitz conducted in 1935 was crucial to the emerging knowledge about the significance of the early mother-child relation. Thus, he demonstrated permanent damage to the child brought about by prolonged separation from or the absence of maternal care and the resulting bodily and emotional under-stimulation. In contradistinction to this, there were no signs of similar injuries or developmental disorders in children who had enjoyed a closer and more continual contact with their mothers.

Like most of the contemporary researchers of his time who were working within this field, Spitz had a background in medicine and psychoanalysis. The research of Spitz and other scientists like John Bowlby, Mary Ainsworth and, later on, Allan Schore decisively changed the methodology and the fundamental mindset of contemporary psychoanalysis by virtue of conducting direct observations and making empirical explorations of the early mother-child relation. With this, the focus was shifted from making theories about the mother-child relation and from making interpretations about what the child's experiences and fantasies meant. Instead, the focus was turned to the reality in which the relation between child and mother unfolds and is created.

The scientific exploration of the human being's physical, mental and emotional coming-into-being during the early attachment between mother and child and in the person's later social relations has revolutionized psychological methodology. To this day, this research continues with the inclusion of still more scientific and social-scientific disciplines like evolutionary biology, neuroscience, developmental psychology, social psychology and sociology. Concurrently, anthropological and cross-cultural studies of human development within indigenous societies and other social systems outside our own cultural area have been carried out.

Finally, observations of higher animals that are closest to human beings are significant for our understanding of the relation between our biological make-up and our need for adequate living conditions, both in early development as well as in the social communities of adulthood. Research within this field can allegedly fortify our understanding of our natural capacity and functioning inasmuch as there seem to be only rather insignificant genetic and biological differences between, for instance, chimpanzees and human beings. Mankind has not changed radically since the Stone Age, notwithstanding the fact that the conditions of our lives have changed considerably since then. The possible consequences of the relation between our natural predisposition and capacity and the current conditions of life is one of the areas this research seeks to illuminate. [89]

Harry Harlow's extensive experiments with rhesus monkeys in the 1950s and 1960s broke new ground within empirical animal research. [90] Harlow demonstrated that young monkeys, beside their basic need for food and safe physical surroundings, also had an equally basic need for caring and for attentive physical and social contact. His experiments proved that a lack of contact with the mother and the social deprivation of young monkeys led to permanent physical, mental, social and emotional injuries, and that the outcome could be fatal. According to Harlow, the cause of death among socially deprived monkeys was emotional anorexia. Whereas researchers working with the studies of the mother-child relation subsequently used the expression, "need for attachment", Harlow spoke about a basic need for love.

Regardless of the fact that Harlow's experiments were the target of criticism because of the damage that the monkeys were subjected to, they have been pivotal in the way we perceive and treat human infants in the early developmental phases. As had Spitz's observations, Harlow's experiments contributed to the crystallization of a completely new perspective on the conditions and methods of child-rearing. Thus, a radical change of child-rearing methods in childcare institutions and at hospitals took place already in the years following the publication of the research results.

A wide spectrum of animal testing research within the fields of biology and neuroscience is presently being conducted in laboratories. Neurobiological processes and the development of the brain are being explored and viewed in relation to, for instance, environmental factors that are either beneficial or harmful to the development of the brain functions, to mental and emotional wellbeing, and to physical health. Studies like these support the clinical observations and the empirical studies insofar as they concretely show what parts of the brain and what aspects of the brain functions develop insufficiently in cases of inadequate care that may be experienced and suffered in the early years of the individual's life.

---

89 Byrnit, 2007
90 Mears, 1985

Attachment theories

John Bowlby grew up in an English upper-class environment in which he, during the years of his early childhood, spent one hour a day with his mother at teatime. In the first four years of his life, a nanny, to whom he became attached as if she were his mother, raised him. When she left the family, he experienced a deeply painful loss that was felt to be along the lines of losing his mother. The reason why upper-class women of the time left the care of their children to the hired nannies was that there was a prevailing consensus that parents supposedly ran the risk of pampering the child when giving it attention and love, thereby causing the child to develop unwanted personality traits.

In Bowlby's groundbreaking report on homeless children's mental health in postwar Europe, the main conclusion he arrived at was that infants and small children have a need to experience a warm, intimate and continual relation with their mothers or caregivers. [91] His findings also show that it is crucial that both parties experience the relationship as rewarding and as a source of joy. According to Bowlby, the absence of this contact could very likely lead to significant and irreversible emotional and mental damage. Bowlby's conclusions were immensely controversial at the time of their publication but they came to exert considerable impact insofar as they contributed, first and foremost – like Spitz's and later Harlow's studies – to changing the conditions of hospitalized and institutionalized children.

Bowlby's report, which resulted from a collation of various case reports about children's physical and psychological developmental disturbances, was met with strong criticism. This criticism was voiced in a clear rejection of Bowlby's conclusion that children need to have a continual and loving relation with their mothers or caregivers in order to develop normally. Doubt was also cast on the premise that this close relation could be said to be a natural and necessary aspect of parenthood – and similarly on the premise that there needs to be a mutually nurturing and rewarding relationship. Furthermore, it was claimed that there was not sufficient evidence in Bowlby's data to draw such conclusions. [92]

---

[91] Bowlby, 1951
[92] Ainsworth, 1962. In 1962, WHO published Deprivation of Maternal Care: A Reassessment of Its Effects with contributions by, e.g., Bowlby's former colleague, Mary Ainsworth. The purpose of publishing this volume was to present the latest research and to correct a number of misconceptions. The publication was also an attempt to compensate for the earlier report's lack of evidence regarding the consequences of lacking parental care.

A political bias was imputed to Bowlby's conclusions: they were regarded as an attempt to scare mothers away from working outside the home and from placing their children in day-care institutions. At the time Bowlby's report was published, there was, in fact, a considerable need for supplying work places with female labor that could secure growth in manufacturing products to get the economy up and running after the war.

Bowlby realized that there was a necessity for a completely new understanding and for new theories in the study of the early development processes of children. [93] He therefore sought insight into and cooperated with research areas within evolutionary biology, ethology, developmental psychology and cognitive sciences. [94] This interest in interdisciplinary research met with sympathy within these research areas and subsequently also among various newly developed research branches in neuroscience and other disciplines.

The formation of theories of attachment that began with Bowlby's observations of the early mother-child relation is still ongoing. These theories deal with the attachment of healthily developed children as well as of mentally and emotionally deviant children. Furthermore, research is being done on the attachment behavior of adults, as it turns out that attachment is seen as a necessary aspect of human self-expression and that it is significant throughout the course of life.

Attachment, exploration, and empathy

With Allan Schore as a seminal figure in the further development of attachment theory, biological research and neuroscience have played increasing roles in this research. In more recent years, attention has been focused on the connection between the mental and emotional state of the child – in his/her interaction with his/her mother or another permanent caregiver – and the make-up and development of the brain in the early developmental process. [95] Schore understands the attachment relation as a combination of psychological predisposition, coded into the individual child, and the interaction experienced with the mother or caregiver. Through close, interdisciplinary studies, it has been demonstrated that it is absolutely essential for the infant and for the development process in the first years, that the child learns through experience, in close and attentive contact with the mother or the primary caregiver, and that the child feels fundamentally related to this person.

---

93 Bowlby, 1988
94 Harlow, 1958. Harlow's experiments with rhesus monkeys were motivated by a wish to give empirical support to Bowlby's view.
95 Schore, 1994

The child's urge for exploration can be observed very early in his/her close contact with the caregiver. This urge for exploration is – by the way – active throughout our entire lifetime. The drive of exploration is considered, within the field of attachment research, just as basic and life-supporting a drive as the drive for the gratification of physical needs. It is in the attentive field of the encounter between the child and the mother that they mutually sense, experience, and discover themselves and each other. If the child is supported and encouraged in this exploration on its own terms – and if this is done with the right timing – the child will develop a sense of being able to empathize with the inner experience of the other and will, at the same time, experience that the other does the same. This capacity for accommodating mutual empathy and compassion is crucial to the child's incipient realization of and knowledge about itself and the world. It is, in the words of Allan Schore, the origin and formation of the self.

The child, in other words, becomes aware and conscious of its own feelings and experiences when the mother recognizes and attunes her emotional expression, bringing it into accord with that of the child. It is also in this relation that the child learns emotional control, since the child is given the opportunity, through the mother's attunement, to learn to adapt and control its effect and emotional behavior and, in time, to express its feelings and behavior in accordance with a clear perception of the situation. [96]

This, in turn, is the basis for the later development of empathy and ethical discernment as well as of ethical attitude and behavior. The child thus experiences, through its capacity for compassion and empathy, that another person experiences discomfort if the child, for instance, should come to inflict pain on the other person. Furthermore, the child discovers and gets in touch with an experience of discomfort when doing this. In a converse way, the child will experience that making another person happy is a source of joy.

The authentic, open and joyful atmosphere between the child and the caregiver in the early process of exploration, empathizing and formation not only generates a feeling of basic trust in the relationship. It is also stands as a precondition to the child's development of a confident perception of him/herself and the world. The child experiences the joy of discovering him/herself and the world and of being-in- the-world. According to Allan Schore, the thrill of exploring and the ability to expe-

---
96 ibid.

rience joy belong to the deeper human functions that come into formation in the child's first years.

Experiences acquired in this contact are crucial to the child's mental and emotional development and to the way that the brain grows in the first two years of the child's life. Both of these advances constitute the foundation for later developmental processes. Apparently, the brain does not automatically grow larger but is organized, disorganized and reorganized in the years of the primary growth period, which extends from three months before until two years after the child's birth. Accordingly, the experiences that the child has had in the relationship with the caregivers and the surrounding environment are crucial to the growth of the brain. This is apparently so because the formation of synapses and neural networks seems to be guided by the principle, "use it or lose it".

Attachment over time
Both the degree and the quality of attachment – and attachment behavior – in the early mother-child relationship and later in life may vary, due to – albeit not exclusively – the caregiver and the surrounding environment. Children are different and will immediately after birth display **temperamental differences and variations in their developmental pace and timing** although generally speaking, children who have a secure attachment will develop a stable and appropriate self-perception and have better opportunities for development, also later on in life, than their peers that have a less secure attachment. Children who have a secure attachment will also display comparatively greater independence, resilience and flexibility in connection with changes and later mental strain and stress.

The fundamental experience of basic trust that characterizes a healthy attachment can, at times, come under pressure. This might happen when significant changes occur in the family matrix or when unexpected or prolonged strains, uncertainty, and stress come to affect the environment during childhood and later in life. Basic trust is not given once and for all and is not necessarily stable over time. The surrounding environment and the circumstances of life can also, later on in childhood and in adult life, affect a person's experience of trust and confidence in relation to him- or herself and the world and thereby also later influence the person's development and maturation.

Attentive empathy and rational manageability
In spite of the comprehensive knowledge we now have about the early mother-child relationship and the influence of childhood conditions on

the formation of a person, notions of earlier times that do not agree with our present knowledge still seem to influence child-rearing and educational practices. This becomes obvious when the child – at the age of six months to one year – is sent into daycare. In the following, a brief account will be given of this as well as an account of the tension of imbalance that can be spotted between, on the one hand, our knowledge about the significance of attentive care and empathy in relation to the individual child and, on the other, principles aiming at rational manageability and the exercise of a generalized targeted effort in relationship to the child's development.

In the period before the intense exploration of the mother-child relation was ushered in, around the time of World War II and in the following couple of decades, it was universally understood that infants primarily require – as a Danish saying goes – "calmness, cleanliness, and consistency". This led to the development of a practice of feeding, changing, giving social contact to and bathing children at fixed times, whereupon they were put back in the cradle, where they – according to the prevailing recommendations – had to remain, regardless of how much they cried. Since children were frequently not breast-fed or were quickly weaned, meals were consumed in the cradle, where the bottle was placed at a comfortable nursing height, propped up so that it would not fall over. This practice was also followed in nurseries, where infants were placed after two to four weeks of maternity leave extended to the working mothers.

When the child was nevertheless picked up by its mother – who was moved by the baby's crying – and the child subsequently initiated contact-seeking behavior, i.e. when the child started babbling happily and contently, it was determined that nothing was wrong with the child and that it *only* wanted attention and company, after which the child was returned to its cradle. If the child promptly started crying again, the prevailing recommendation was for the caregiver to remove oneself as far as possible from the place where the child was laying so that one would not be affected by the crying. The line of reasoning was that the child needed to get into its resting and sleeping rhythm and this was further buttressed by the fact that the child eventually fell asleep. Many people who grew up during the heyday of this child-rearing method can confirm that they, as children, often experienced how it feels to "cry oneself to sleep".

The approach toward practicing the aforementioned ideals of care is rather typical of a rational mindset, characterized by its tendency to perceive reality with a sense of the generalized and purpose-oriented. Hereby, what initially appear to be perfectly reasonable considerations regarding certain basic needs of infants can be systematized: manageability, harmonization and product-oriented goal achievement can be translated into concrete frameworks and guidelines for caregivers. Attentive empathy and meeting the individual child in its own right are easily disregarded and dismissed as if they were neither of importance to the child nor of any importance to the caregiver.

During the past centuries, a multitude of ideas and opinions about the position of children has been articulated and a broad spectrum of socialization methodologies has been developed and practiced. These include both the abovementioned "calmness, cleanliness, and consistency" method, replete with its notion of a firm hand in disciplining and raising the children, and the contrasting attitude of being open to an interactive exchange between child and caregiver, in accordance with the individual needs and development process of the child.

Today, a kaleidoscopic picture of opinions and practices seems to coexist, with the envisioned methodologies positioned in parallel with each other. The gradual extension of maternity leave, which, for the time being, grants Danish parents the right to spend one year at home with their child, complies with recent research results about the importance of early close and intimate care. The rigid pedagogy in nurseries and kindergartens has also been replaced by a greater understanding of the individual needs of a child who is undergoing the processes of physical, psychological, and mental development.

In the last decades, however, it has increasingly become more widespread and more generally accepted that children from an early age in nurseries and in their schooling are subjected to educational teaching plans, coupled with evaluation and control measures in order to secure a uniform and goal-fulfilling development process. With this, there is a real risk that the understanding of and respect for individual differences as well as the considerations that development does *not* progress linearly are all being neglected. Increasingly more demands related to goal-fulfillment and the reporting of development objectives give rise to the risk of dampening teachers' own free exploration of and empathic insight into the real needs of the child. This tendency will invariably limit individual teachers' free and spontaneous exercise of pedagogical practice that might prove to be appropriate to the situation.

It is evidently difficult to pursue and adapt the general understanding of the young child's need for attentive care and individual learning, transpiring in dynamical interaction with the caregiver, into the growing child's continued development and learning processes. A markedly abrupt transition from the recommended empathic closeness in the child's first years to the increasingly goal-oriented learning in nurseries and kindergartens and further on in the child's school education bears witness to this. Invariably, we are left with the impression that:

> *the more civilized we perceive ourselves to be and the more dominated we are by an overriding   political-economic mindset, the farther we are removing ourselves from our natural ground as caregivers and guides of our children and adolescents.*

The generally widespread uncertainty that can be spotted among those whose task it is to be primary caregiver – that is, the parents – is perhaps the most convincing testimony to this.

The social Implications of attachment theories

Allan Schore has no doubt that attachment theories and the comprehensive knowledge that has been gathered over the last 40-50 years potentially have far-reaching social implications. At the same time, he is worried about the meager degree of attention that this knowledge actually receives and how few societal resources are being allotted to this area in comparison to, for instance, what is allotted for the defense budget, which supposedly is what will secure our lives now and in the future.

For Schore, there is no doubt that it is the coming generation that constitutes the greatest asset for bringing about a meaningful, healthy and safe world. In an interview with Roz Carroll, [97] **Schore argues that children are capable of forming concepts about the self and of forming both positive and negative perceptions of the self. Children display empathy and learn self-regulation and develop the ability to read other peoples' states of mind. These skills, according to Schore, are formed during the early interaction with the primary caregiver and are not the result of the later formation and acquisition of language. On its part, this is the very basis for the development of skills and the maturing of human competencies and qualities. Thus, although he hesitates to call it scandalous, Schore points out that, at any rate, it is really a shame that adequate funds are not being invested and that competent teachers are not being trained to socialize and educate children adequately from an early age.**

---
97 Carroll, 2012

Being and development

In the following exposition of A.H. Almaas's observations of and theory about the early mother-child interaction, light will be shed on more subtle aspects of development in childhood. [98] What will furthermore be elucidated is how these may come to influence the development of potentials and qualities in the process of maturation in adulthood.

Like the abovementioned attachment theorists, Almaas is inspired by the object relations theory found in psychoanalytic psychology. [99] In the first six months of the child's life – the symbiotic phase – the child is assumed to be in a state of being in the totality in which it exists. According to Almaas, the mutual empathy, which occurs between mother and child in this phase, is primarily due to the mother's ability to experience a resonance of the state of being that the child is in, so that she, in company with the child, experiences and explores this space and the various experiential qualities that gradually unfurl, spontaneously.

This state is experienced by both the child and the mother as a feeling of being in a blissful union. The experience of being in this undivided state of unity is initially without reference to time, space and concepts. Within this state of inseparable and undivided being, the feeling of being existentially embraced, supported and *held* is, according to Almaas, the very foundation for the development of basic trust in the child – just as it is the mother's chance of actualizing and re-experiencing this feeling. [100]

In the course of the first year, it is possible to observe the child's expression of an increasing variation of qualities and emotional states such as sorrow and joy, trust, anger, strength, will power, love, curiosity, creativity, intelligence and vitality. The better the child is supported and appreciated in this initial and spontaneous expression of potentials and qualities, and the better the child, during the formation of the self and personality, is guided in expressing these qualities, the better the child is

---

[98] Almaas, 2000
[99] A theory about the development of the psychological structure of the "I", which was developed by, e.g., Harry Guntrip, Donald D. Winnicott, Margaret Mahler, Otto F. Kernberg and Heinz Kohut.
[100] Davidson & Harrington, 2001. Findings from recent brain research seem to support the assumption that there are certain similarities between the infant's experience of existing within an indistinct being and the experiences that adult test subjects report when they, during meditation, are experiencing a state of undisturbed and attentive presence.
(20) This presentation on inner estrangement and alienation builds on Almaas, (2000), on Levine, (1997) and on my own work as a social scientist and trauma psychologist. This has been published in the following works: Praetorius, (2002), (2004), (2007) and (2013).

able to develop basic trust and achieve an authentic self-perception and adequate self-esteem.

The development of an authentic self-perception means that the child gets to know him or herself as an inner sensed experience. The child will furthermore develop the ability to discern between what it is to be genuine and authentic, to be oneself, as opposed to what is experienced as being strange and inauthentic.

Conversely, if the child is *not* supported and appreciated or if the child is ignored or perhaps even rejected or punished for the spontaneous expression of its qualities like joy, love, strength and will power, the child will eventually develop an experience of being wrong. Maybe the caregivers have scant contact with these qualities in themselves and are therefore unable to accommodate the child or perhaps they cannot embrace the child's spontaneous expression. Perhaps they feel that the child expresses its qualities differently from the ways that they themselves would have. The child will gradually, in the course of its first year, get the impression that "when I am who am I, in my way, I am wrong". And because the child is fundamentally dependent on the physical and emotional care and appreciation obtained from its primary caregiver, the child begins to distance itself from its own contact with its qualities and their natural expression. Instead, the child is forced to learn and to imitate a way of experiencing him/herself that he/she has been led to believe is what the caregiver wants and expects. Hence the child distorts its spontaneous and natural way of experiencing and expressing itself. The child is, in other words, pushed into experiencing and expressing itself in ways that secure acceptance of its surroundings.

This is consistent with the observations of the attachment theorists: the child will seek attachment regardless of the conditions and the quality of contact and interaction with the primary caregivers. Attachment is, in other words, so important for the child's coming-into-being in the world that it will put up with whatever is offered and simply adapt to the given conditions.

Survival strategies and inner estrangement

In the first years, the child's identity and personality formation is guided and determined by an external guidance and control which, to varying degrees, respects the child's uniqueness and potentials. Gradually, the child will internalize this external guidance and control in the form of mental and emotional formations that aim at shaping the child's development in accordance with the expectations and demands of the surroundings. Hence the child will seek to obtain recognition from important caregivers in order and avoid disapproval and punishment.

If the child receives inadequate recognition and acceptance, he/she is forced – to a greater or lesser extent – to develop a distorted identity and to develop fear-based survival strategies.

The survival strategies are mental formations arising out of a state of fear and powerlessness that occur when being rejected for simply being "who I am".

These survival strategies will fixate the child – and later the adult – in an inflexible and gradually unrealized surveillance and regulation of attitude and behavior. In other words, the child can lose the freedom to choose, think and act authentically as well as the freedom to be true to itself. The mental formation of the survival strategies will be incorporated in the child's perception of self and the world. When such survival strategies and the associated mental and emotional thought structures become integrated parts of the child's personality formation and self-perception, a double shattering of the child's unique individuality and natural expression occurs: at first, through the caregiver's rejection and subsequently, through the self-rejection of the child.

The child's rejection of and separation from the contact with its being, with its qualities and with their natural expression is a painful process and leaves a void of deep inadequacy, with concomitant feelings of distrust, anxiety, frustration, sorrow, anger and depression. According to Almaas, existential human pain and anxiety spring from this process.

It is, figuratively speaking, on top of this void – the so-called "deficient emptiness", in which something crucial is missing – that the child develops its personality structure and experience of identity. Depending on the extent to which the child has had an opportunity to retain some semblance of authentic contact with itself and its qualities, its personality structure will be marked by a greater or lesser degree of the rigidity that is characteristic of inauthentic identity and survival strategies.

> Deficient contact with and inadequate development of one's own authentic qualities characterize the state of "inner estrangement".

This state may not be a conscious one. But later on in life it can, from time to time, manifest itself in the form of feelings of inner emptiness and inadequacy related to experiencing and expressing oneself: "I am really something more than I appear to be but it's as if something is preventing me from expressing it" or "I have to become better, because deep down, I know that I have more to offer".

Conversely, attentiveness to and respect for the child's unique individuality and development process will, under favorable conditions of development, enhance the child's natural self-confidence and fortify his/her sense of trust and of being independent in relation to his/her surroundings. The child will develop a healthy feeling of being and a solid sense of being able to express itself adequately and will stand firmly on its own ground.

Alienation and traumatization in the personality formation
Inner estrangement and externally determined alienation can be formulated in the following ways:

1. When the child is cut off from its own unique qualities, its abilities and its natural expression, the child will suffer from inner estrangement.

2. When the child is furthermore forced to identify with externally imposed ways of perceiving and expressing him- or herself, the child is undergoing a process of being alienated to him- or herself. To be alienated is to identify with an externally determined, distorted and inauthentic self-perception and to think, feel, and act according to this distorted view.

3. The condition of inner estrangement and the condition externally determined alienation encompass a sense of deficiency, anxiety, anger, and depression.

Insufficient attention to and recognition of the child as being a unique person will, in serious cases, be experienced by the child as overwhelming, inescapable and insurmountable. This unsatisfactory deficiency leaves the child with an experience of impotence, anxiety, sorrow and anger because it feels incapable of doing anything that might change the situation or alter the conditions. The experience of being at a loss and of giving up is a deep and painful feeling that, to a greater or lesser extent, becomes embedded in the early formation of the human personality. This experience is associated with guilt and shame, suffered partly for not living up to the expectations and demands of the surroundings and partly from being forced to reject that which is felt to be genuine and precious within oneself.

In the process of developing inner estrangement and externally determined alienation, the child will consciously or unconsciously experience being existentially threatened. In severe cases, a state of traumatization due to the fear of being annihilated psychologically will become manifest as neurobiological high stress. This can, over time, become embedded as a latent, chronic high stress condition. [101]

In Chapter 3, alienation was elucidated as one way in which human beings are being conceptualized by leading social and management theories, which are formulating and managing human beings and their lives as though they were things. Thus alienation, in this case, can be said to be the process by which adult human beings, as the result of a reifying view and externally formed notions of the person, are being forced to think, feel, and act in ways that are fundamentally alien to themselves.

The resultant latent, chronic high-stress condition and the survival strategies may give rise to disorders in the personality formation. These can display themselves, in both children and adults, as psychological imbalances like depression and anxiety and, in even more serious cases, as disorders that characterize the narcissistic and borderline personality disorder.

Personal emancipation as maturation process
A potentially invasive and undermining child-rearing method that encourages external control of the child's development process takes its point of departure in a quid-pro-quo ("something for something") mindset and in the "consequence thinking" of the educators. It rests on the underlying application of principles like "If you don't do as I want, I have the power and the means to withhold what you need" and "You have to earn my care, love, and recognition by being as – and by doing what – I want you to". This mindset and its consequences are then transferred to the child. In return for being as and doing what caregivers and other authority figures want him/her to do, the child enters into an (unholy) alliance with them and develops strategies whereby it believes it can haggle to obtain *Ersatz*-gratification instead of a real but apparently not always achievable feeling of closeness, care, acceptance and recognition.

> It is noteworthy that the inhabitants of Mungiki consider the mindset that is seated behind these kinds of child-rearing principles as being cruel and as a sign of lack of love for the children.

---

101 Praetorius, 2014

Depending on the conditions in our childhood, we are all marked by the experience of an upbringing that, to a greater or lesser degree, is authority-based and which may, at that, have been invasive and undermining. The adult's personal emancipation and maturation process is comprised of a gradual confrontation with and dissolution of these imprints of childhood. The distorted and acquired perception of oneself and of the world that has been spawned by external alienation and inner estrangement will come to be challenged and will gradually loosen its grip. In the course of the maturation process of adulthood, we get to know ourselves and we get a chance to reestablish contact with the lost land in ourselves: our own being, our qualities and existential values, and our unique way of expressing ourselves.

The human maturation process could be said to depend on our continual calling into question our identity, our perception of the world, and our view of life. For many people, this occurs already in childhood and continues throughout life – albeit in what is sometimes a more or less unnoticed way.

There are, however, certain periods in our lives when we are naturally confronted with existential queries and we need to reconsider and reorient our notion of who we are and in what manner life give meaning and makes sense to us. Accordingly, existential questions have a tendency to come into focus in periods of transition from one age-phase to another. Such weighty questions can also be triggered by events and occurrences that crucially change the course of somebody's life – for instance, when confronted with illness, the death of a close relative, unemployment or divorce.

Puberty marks an age where most of us will question our identity and self-perception. The first serious confrontation with an externally determined alienation of the personality takes place and an attempt is made to find oneself behind a distorted identity. This is, in reality, an incredibly courageous confrontation because the young person is not only revolting against the people who have been – and still are - caregivers and safeguards. He or she is furthermore embarking on a journey into an existential, mental, and emotional no-man's-land, into the unknown, while staking his/her familiar identity and self-perception.

Any particular phase in which existential choices come into focus could be said to be a repetition of the confrontation of identity, the search for meaning, and the emancipation of one's teenage years at ever higher levels of progression. These periods of life are necessary for a person's maturation and for his/her emancipation from both the externally determined alienation and the inner estrangement.

In the process of maturation, we, as adult persons, have the choice of increasingly being true to ourselves and of being self-reliant. Authentic self-perception and sense of self thus depend on a progressive developmental process, whereby both the externally determined alienation and the inner estrangement are weakened. Henceforth, the person's potentials and qualities may mature more freely and unfold in a mutually enriching exchange with the social, educational, and work-related communities. This process is supported, for instance, when we are faced, in the years of our youth, with challenges that can be met and when we are able to rise to the occasion of facing up to the challenges during the educational and working life of adulthood. In other words: social matrices like peer groups during puberty and, later on in life, work-related experiences transpiring in groups of colleagues can be powerful agents in diminishing the negative effects of adversities suffered in early childhood. [102]

The societally relevant human being

The ideal of the market society comprised of societally relevant human beings and the methods applied in managing and controlling and the methods applied in the evaluation of the development, learning, and maturation process all bear striking likenesses with the previously mentioned authoritarian and invasive upbringing of the child. It leaves both the child, and later the adult, who is subjected to this kind of management, in a situation where he or she, due to his/her dependency on the authority, is forced to enter into contracts in order to gain acceptance and avoid expulsion. The child, as well as the adult, is left in a situation in which he/she has to bargain in order to retain the (vitally) necessary affiliation and be rewarded in exchange for developing a societally adapted personality and performance.

The continued alienating and potentially traumatizing subversion of the natural maturation process runs the risk of preventing the adult from being able to dilute and dissolve the distorted identifications and negative imprints of the early development process. There is, on the contrary, a definite risk that these identifications and imprints are being reinforced. This manifests itself, with regrettable conspicuousness, in the increasing number of psychological and physical imbalances and disorders that

---
102 Rutter, 2002

are being suffered later in life by otherwise normal and healthy people. Furthermore, completely new and serious psychological disorders have especially emerged in children and adolescents. [103]

Today, there is a tendency to consider it inconvenient when other people show signs of being at a stage in life where existential questions and identity crises are in focus. People in such situations will invariably experience doubt and insecurity and will be questioning familiar notions, attitudes, and ways of acting in the world. Perhaps they are accordingly not as streamlined and productive as is ordinarily demanded in our highly effective society, where our performance is constantly being evaluated and where questions and considerations about existential matters that might give meaning to us are not ascribed much significance. From time to time, what could be taken to be altogether natural and necessary states in a person's ongoing maturation process – and maybe because they are not perceived or appreciated as being natural and necessary – may develop into life crises, in which the person develops signs of genuine mental instability. For these states, we have diagnostic categories and a long range of treatments, ranging from medication to different kinds of therapy that are designed to serve the purpose of getting the person "back on the 'right' track".

The ethical challenge of our time

Taking our vast knowledge about the functioning, development and education of human beings into account, we could ask:

- Are we presently about to create the best of worlds? Or are we, paradoxically enough, currently in the process of globally giving rise to dehumanization and alienation on a scale that is unprecedented in the history of mankind?

- How can we handle the immense ethical challenge that an increasing number of citizens in our growth-through-competition societies are developing fear-based survival strategies which undermine a healthy personality formation and the healthy maturation of human qualities?

Becoming reduced and alienated in the hopes of getting a share of the economic and material growth and simultaneously being exposed to the threat of either conforming or being dismissed is the predicament

---
103 Mithen, 1996

that rests heavily upon human beings of our time. Thus, among the most powerful deceptions being proliferated by the current market society is the dogma that competition – on all levels of society and between nations – is necessary in order to survive. This is a dogma that implies that survival is a matter of "me or them". It is deceitful in that it has been able to overshadow the truth that it is the ability and the natural urge of human beings to collaborate empathically while expressing uniquely human qualities and values that have made it possible for humanity to survive as a species under widely different conditions of life. [104]

Life on Mungiki is definitely not Heaven on Earth and the Mungikis are human beings just like the rest of us. They do not possess the knowledge and educational resources of our contemporary societies. The people living there do, however, embody the wisdom that acknowledges our mutual interdependency, which is essential in forming sustainable communities that are in harmony with the surrounding nature. This manifests itself in their mutual cooperation – from an early age – and where everybody counts in collecting, distributing and sharing the means of sustenance on their island – because they know full well that it is a matter of survival. [105]

No human being can survive without being attended to or without participating him/herself in the communities and cultures that we create together and live in. Perhaps the best we can do for ourselves and our children is to face up to the challenge it is to manage and pass on the very best about ourselves as human beings. We have already gained vitally important knowledge about the effect of mutual empathic relations on the early personality formation. Acquiring further knowledge about the adult person's development of human potentials and about how empathy matures into ethical attitudes and compassionate behavior might turn out to be one of the decisive preconditions for the survival of humanity in the future.

---

104 Mithen, 1996
105 Christiansen, 1975

CHAPTER 6
IN PURSUIT OF THE AUTHENTIC

Existential considerations and reflections often spring from an urge to examine whether the world we are creating is really the best we can muster. In this chapter, we will pursue different trails in order to seek knowledge about our human nature and the conditions of existence. We will deal especially with the question about whether certain conditions of life, more than others, promote the development of humanitarian attitudes and humanitarian ways of living.

The chapter begins with considerations of how we can locate and pin down the concept of authenticity. Then light will be shed on scientific research that deals with the origin and genesis on both micro as well as on macro level - from the smallest entities to the whole universe - and how we understand evolution. Our being in the world in our own culture will be examined and seen in the light of my own experiences of living in an indigenous culture. These reflections will be related to quantum physics. Throughout the exposition, and in the following chapters we will continually reflect on how a progression in ethical thinking and conduct can take place in our time.

Who do we want to be?

The search for authenticity and for becoming the person we truly are rests on the assumption that we actually hold unexplored and still rather unrealized potentials and that we, in the process of letting go of the distortions of our perception of self, are capable of realizing a healthier and fuller expression of who we are.

Regardless of how counterproductive our habitual notions and identifications might be and regardless of how much pain these can cause, from time to time, in our own life and in that of others, it is incredibly difficult to let go of what is distorted and that which causes the distortion. Based on what is experienced i.e. within the field of psychotherapy, the giving up of old, distorted patterns depends on being able to replace them with what in the course of the process is realized to be a truer perspective on who we are and basically want to be.

In Chapter 5, the small child's process of becoming was shown to rely on the child's urge to explore and discover the unfolding of its personality in an ongoing contact with close caregivers. This exploration supports the development of basic trust and the feeling of empathy in relation to self and the surrounding world. This, in turn, is found to be a necessary condition for the child to explore and develop its unique potentials and qualities. The innate capacity to explore and be curious, to reflect and to empathize is also crucial to the ongoing maturation and development of qualities and potentials in the adolescent and in the adult. For a process of maturation to be actualized and brought to expression, it is crucial that the person has the courage to question, reflect on, and rethink him- or herself and the world on the basis of perspectives that are different from the acquired ones.

Individuation – Independence – Authenticity
The ideas, thoughts, and attitudes we have about ourselves and the world around us rely on the interplay between internal and external conditions, thus forming a holistic view which imparts a sense of coherence and meaning to existence. Thus, an ongoing dependent relation of causation takes place between the particular person's unique potentials and biological and genetic make-up, the immediate environment and whatever historical, cultural and social conditions prevail at the given time.

The process of individuation, where the person develops and matures into his or her own natural preconditions and potentials as an independent individual, is the very formation of the person as an authentic individual. It is a progressing process of being empowered to live and act in tune with what is experienced as being personally true and of value, and that makes sense. An authentic person being confidently and empathetically present can be distinguished by openness, spontaneity and flexibility in relation to him/herself and others.

Authentic individuality differs in many respects from the personality formation that was labeled "conformist individualism" in Chapter 4. A person developing conformist individualism will tend to fixate and close individuality up around themself. The capacity for exploring confidently and empathetically into oneself and the surroundings runs the risk of being superimposed upon and replaced by laborious efforts to figure out what image and what narrative about myself and my performance will be seen as successful in the situation right now and for which I will be recognized and rewarded by the surroundings. [106]

Authentic individuality is found in a person who is capable of maintaining his/her integrity and simultaneously remaining aware of others in the situations and circumstances of life in which the person finds him/herself. Authentic individuality is expressed in the person's ability to be present as him/herself in various situations in life and with different kinds of people – of different social backgrounds and attitudes – while simultaneously being open to exploring and learning from his/her meetings with others. Such a person, seems, in other words to be trustworthy and is seen as the embodiment of the classical humanistic ideal of education.

The ethical dilemma of the individual

Regardless of the degree to which we might be subjected to externally determined limitations, we nevertheless hold what is necessary to break with the alienation and distorted perception of self and the world of conformist individualism. It is not necessary to have extraordinary abilities and qualities and to be an exceptional person; authentic individuality is not an ideal for the exceptional few or an ideal mental construction but rather a reality that we can all experience in our own individual ways. As a citizen, and in my capacity as a psychologist and supervisor in our own society, and as a cross-cultural researcher in non-Western societies, I have had the privilege of meeting people who managed - no matter how difficult conditions they were subject to and worked under - to uphold their integrity and meet others openly and with genuine compassion.

Appreciating the authentic person is possible, because he or she strikes a similar chord within us. Being inspired of such a person to make changes ourselves is not a question of breaking any natural laws but rather of abstaining from following conventions that support certain historically determined political-economic understanding of society and humanity that has proven to be counterproductive to the natural expression, sanity and the communal life of humanity. Because there is very little to indicate that there is any political will to consider and discuss this issue, it

---

106 Neufeld and Maté, (2005). Neufeld and Maté shed light on a range of developmental disorders that occur in children today and which are the result in cases when children, from an early age – due to the fragmented and stressed-out life lived by their parents as well as to the insufficient staffing of qualified daycare workers and teachers – are forced to fend for themselves without sufficiently attentive relationships with adults. The children are consequently forced to orient their attachment in daycare institutions and schools toward their peers, who are just as immature as they are themselves. According to the writers, these children develop a pronounced conformism. And it is likely that this conformism will tend to characterize the person later in life.

might be more realistic to assume that a change of perspective is going to depend on people's considerations and initiative to individually and collectively make personal choices based on each individual's resources and readiness.

The dilemma that confronts us is that we, on the one hand – by choosing to adapt to the societal preconditions out of loyalty to the communities we are part of – risk losing ourselves and our credibility. And, on the other hand, that we – by choosing to be true to ourselves based on the wish to be in the world as independent and authentic human beings – are making this choice without any guarantees that we are going to be rewarded. The pressing questions are who each of us wants to be and how important it is to us to be true to ourselves.

In the following, we will reflect upon some historically and culturally determined notions and views that dominate how we, having been so deeply influenced by the age of the cult of rationality in the Western world, see ourselves and the world. Also, perceptions and language usage stemming from cultures other than our own – perceptions and language usage that exhibit a more varied perception of self and reality – will be presented. We will furthermore reflect on whether and to what degree mechanistic physics and the more recent research within quantum mechanics influence our perception of ourselves and reality.

Who do we think we are?

Throughout the history of human life on the planet, we have continually left behind a richly varied and ongoing testimony about the various notions we have had about the universe and Earth. Creation stories, tales, myths, legends, images, sculptures, sound and dance are all concrete expressions of our different notions about human life, its origin, expression and cessation.

In our time, these have long since come to be supplanted by scientific studies of life and the conditions of existence on Earth. Ongoing research covers a vast spectrum of the manifestations of life – ranging from the smallest biological building blocks to explorations on the larger scale undertaken by geologists, archeologists, anthropologists and historians. In addition to this, in recent years, astrophysicists have been exploring and mapping out space and the heavenly bodies and the relations between the phenomena of the cosmos. In order to account for the myriad of dynamic, multidimensional and incessantly changing phenomena, we presently make use of complex mathematical models that serve to support theories which increasingly challenge and surpass human comprehension.

The paradox, however, is that the ongoing research within the fields of mathematics and modern quantum physics, as well as in the field of astrophysics, apparently adds unfathomable dimensions and new mysteries to reality and existence. Furthermore, even within exact sciences like physics and mathematics, research is based on assumptions that cannot be proven and interdependent relations that hardly lend themselves to being formulated.

The question, however, is: has our urge to know still more about ourselves, our history and the space of existence – by primarily studying what exists and unfolds in physical space and the processes that take place in the human organism – actually brought us onto the trail of hitherto unknown areas of humanity and existence?

What do we mean by "evolution"?

Research on the development of the human species generally springs from the assumption that humanity has gone through, and is still undergoing, a process of *evolving* which has taken us, in the course of millions of years, from the animal realm to our present state as human beings. We might reflect upon the question of whether these studies have resulted in findings that show that we are still in a progressive process of development and evolution. Or whether the more moderate optimism of progress, declaring that humanity – generation by generation – learns and becomes wiser, will prove correct when we use this historical perspective.

After the great world wars, international organizations were founded for the purpose of preventing any more wars. Out of respect for every human being on Earth, conventions have been drawn up and adopted for the purpose of minimizing human suffering and inequality in the world. These measures, as well as the tireless efforts of many people working on many levels within a wide range of various institutions all over the world, have indubitably contributed to raising awareness about the importance of fostering basic ethical values and human rights. In most parts of the world, there is a general consensus that it is necessary to be guided by humanistic ideas and realize them in practice in order to create a world in peaceful coexistence.

It is, however, the *realization* of the ideas that seems to be in such short supply, and especially the farther away from the concrete reality we happen to find ourselves. It is as if the ideas are inevitably considered to be necessary for progression to happen but that they are, time and again, overridden. This takes place especially clearly on the level of management – and apparently for purposes of securing power over national and economic interests. For instance, on the pretext that we – as long as the other side fails to observe and realize these ideas – are operating well within our right when we make exceptions in concrete situations. So, that which should otherwise make us act, right here and now, to create a better world, which would be based on ethical thinking and a deeper understanding of humanity, is paradoxically being postponed until sometime in the future, *after* the world has already become a better place. And maybe this is because we, by that time, will have achieved the necessary position and power to secure ourselves in the best possible way.

Today, we tend to believe that human intelligence has expanded in light of the development of information and knowledge as well as by virtue of the development of competencies applied in the production of technology and communication. The question, though, is whether we, in the course of time and at the same tempo, have developed those areas of our intelligence that deal with our ability to take care of ourselves, each other and our physical conditions of life. We could, for instance, ask whether we have taken into account the motives for and the consequences of our intelligent inventiveness. As has been pointed out earlier, it might appear that we are actually witnessing a step backward and a growing human impoverishment. Research within technology and medicine has apparently brought relief to our lives and has contributed to prolonging life expectancy but at the same time we are witnessing an explosive increase in certain physical and psychological maladies that appear to be on the verge of a virtually epidemic spread in the Western World. [107]

It is tempting to ask whether we have any reason to trust that we, as human beings, can take care of our further evolution. Right now, it seems very likely that nature, with its mechanisms of selection, is going to be the driving force in the coming evolution of mankind.

There is a real dilemma here, for if we cannot put our faith in the progressive process of the development of humanity, how can we substantiate the notion of growth and progress that is part and parcel of the basic concept of the Western era of enlightenment and which is such a crucially driving force in our own age?

---

107 Source: WHO

If we, on the other hand, do have faith in the notion of the forward progression of the human evolutionary process, then this faith appears to be incongruous with our lack of awareness of the necessity to develop a greater sense of responsibility and a greater capacity to take care of our living conditions and our fellow human beings. Without spurning what we have been capable of with the aid of rational thought, science and the technological revolution, the time seems to be right for openly – and without preconceived ideas – questioning whether what we have achieved until now in itself is a sign of progress for humanity. We could, for instance, broaden our perspective of what it is to be a human being by turning to the experiences and ways of life spotted in cultures other than our own and looking back on the history of humanity. Yet, maybe most importantly, we might be inspired to inquire into still rather unexplored areas of our consciousness and inquire into the mind's ability to think, analyze, reflect and gain insight.

We know from experience that an unknown context can be truly inspirational and can present openings for asking completely new questions – or for asking questions that we have not thought of asking before. In encountering that which is different, we have the option of being confronted – as was shown in Chapter 5 – with mental frames of reference and values that collide with our own. On reflection, we might even come to realize that what is different is not so strange, after all, but rather a matter of hitherto unnoticed aspects of our reality and perception hereof.

It is in no way the purpose of this book to emphasize the attitudes and behavior of earlier times or to posit ideals while calling the reader's attention to the ability of cultures other than our own to successfully manage the common good. Yet, something different and indigenous will in the following be brought into focus with the intension to consider whether we have forgotten or abstained from developing crucial aspects of the human potential and neglected a progression in ethical ways of living. Not in order to become better at realizing a moderate optimism for the future but rather to awaken an irresistible force to seriously meet the challenges of the times and realize values, attitudes and ways of life that are indispensable for the continuation of life on Earth.

If that is what we want?

An indigenous culture

In Chapter 5, the early socialization practices of our society were compared to the socialization practices of the indigenous culture of Mungiki. In the original field study, my findings on Mungiki brought to attention certain problematic attitudes and practices found in our own society's methods of child rearing, education and management. Perhaps the following story about the Mungikis' perception of the origin of life will likewise spur reflection. The point is whether the rational scientific and, in our own eyes, "superior" ways of reasoning and creating knowledge imply that we base our experience of reality on correct and sufficiently adequate observations. Are we considerably less dependent on handed-down faith and on our trust in authorities' descriptions and statements about reality than, for instance, the dwellers in a faraway indigenous and isolated community in Polynesia? And is our knowledge the result of asking the right questions?

> *During my field study on Mungiki in 1968, I had taken on the task – in addition to making my own research – of confirming or disproving previous findings obtained by a male researcher, findings that stemmed from numerous interviews with the male inhabitants of the island.* [108] *The men of Mungiki had univocally stated that up until the end of the Second World War, when British civil servants and missionaries arrived on the island, the Mungikis did not know about the connection between intercourse and pregnancy. For a male scientist to discuss this subject with the women was considered taboo. It was, however, assumed that women, who are undeniably in closer contact with the biology of conception and pregnancy, were actually more knowledgeable than the men. It thus became my task – being the first female Western woman on the island – to get the women's own views on the matter.*
>
> *My interview took place with women who were raised and had children before the truth of the matter was made known to the Mungikis. We were inside the hut of the oldest woman on Mungiki. In the hut were gathered five or six other middle-aged women, who had come from villages all over the island. It was not without some degree of excitement that I summoned them to hear their stories of the origin of life and to hear what notions and ideas they had entertained about how women get pregnant.*
>
> *My several hours long interview brought nothing new to light. Just as the men, the women allegedly had no knowledge of the causal rela-*

---

108 Historian of religion and anthropology, professor, Ph.D. Torben Monberg

tion between intercourse and pregnancy. They were well aware of all the signs of pregnancy such as the discontinuation of menstruation, the tensing of the breasts, morning sickness, and the occasional predilection for certain foods but these signs and pregnancy itself were the result of their husbands' prayers to the gods to plant the fruit of a child in their wife's womb. During pregnancy, the women observed a specific diet that would benefit the "fruit" in their bellies and they took care to avoid strenuous labor that might lead to miscarriage or premature delivery – in which case the child was being returned to the gods to be planted once again inside the woman on a later occasion.

No matter how much care I took to ask questions that would reveal that they nonetheless knew about the connection between intercourse and pregnancy, I was just given the same answer: children were gifts from the gods who were answering the prayers of the husband. The few cases in which a young woman who was not yet married got pregnant were taken as a sign of gratitude and appreciation from the gods toward the woman's family. [109]

When I mentioned the possible resemblance between the child, its father, its mother, or somebody else in the family, the women claimed that they had not noticed or paid any attention to this.

Nor had they given any consideration to how animals or fish procreate. Before the white man arrived on the island, there were no large animals on Mungiki. So the islanders had not had any opportunity to see animals mate. My continued questioning to make them reveal that they had at least wondered how animals procreate was met by something midway between resignation and wonder at my persistent urge to ask. Animals had offspring. Period!

To the Mungikis, sex was a lovely and joyous game in which they took part relatively freely – although not in the presence of others and never with close relatives or in-laws. From time to time, they were also together sexually with partners with whom they were not married. However, this lustful side of existence had nothing to do with getting children.

It had taken the women several years to grasp the explanation put forth by people from the outside world, and it still did not mean any-

---

[109] Observations presented by other anthropological writers point to a widespread occurrence of youth infertility in indigenous societies and indicate that women do not get pregnant until the age of 18 to 20, that is, until after they get married. See Monberg, 1975.

thing to them. The oldest woman was still not convinced. In the case of the other women, they had come to terms with the explanation. Here, the missionaries came to their aid because the missionaries had told them that children are a gift from God in heaven, so now it was instead to this god that the husband prayed when he wanted his wife to become pregnant. [110]

What good are questions?

The interview took place at a time in which prominent cultural anthropologists were engaged in a vehement debate about whether it could be true that people in some of the world's cultures were ignorant about the physiological role of men in procreation. In opposition to Melford Spiro, Edmund Leach thus believed that such a supposition was highly unlikely and ran counter to common sense. [111] He adamantly opposed the use of the term "ignorance" in this context as it, in his view, indicated that people in the culture in question were childish, stupid and superstitious.

But is ignorance necessarily an expression of immaturity and of lack of logical and rational thought?

Perhaps, what is surprising is not so much the "ignorance" of the Mungikis as the fact that it surprises us. If nothing else, we are reminded that ignorance, just as well as knowledge, is relative, that is to say, situational. The question is whether the Mungikis are so crucially different from us when we take into account that the considerable knowledge we have acquired, the truth of which we do not doubt, is based to a very large extent on blind faith in research results that we do not have a ghost of a chance to verify or even so much as grasp the truth of by means of our rational intelligence.

We know, for instance, that physical objects, on certain levels of description within physics, are said to be composed of atoms and molecules in perpetual motion. We also know that conception occurs when a sperm cell meets an egg. Even so, most of us have not had the opportunity ourselves to make the observations that led to this knowledge and we have therefore not had any opportunity to verify the findings. Nonetheless, we are willing to believe that knowledge, being the result of scientific research, is correct and we are inclined to believe that it is in accordance with this belief that we know ourselves and the world and that we act accordingly.

---

110 See Praetorius-Israel & Monberg, 1971; Monberg, 1975
111 Spiro, 1966. Leach, 1969

But is this really the case?

If we know that intercourse can cause conception, why do we not use this knowledge and our ability to think rationally to prevent conception when we don't want pregnancy to occur? And why are we inclined, here in Denmark, to believe that a not always risk-free abortion procedure is a right that women should have because it ensures that women can freely decide over their own bodies? In cases where both the woman and the man consensually and freely take part in the act that leads to pregnancy, then both the woman and the man already have the full freedom to decide over their own bodies – or what? This sequence of arguments is not a contribution to the debate for or against the free choice of abortion, but merely a reflection on whether we, in any situation, are thinking and acting as rationally as we are inclined to believe.

Already in school, we are taught science and learn that physical objects on the subatomic level, according to the most recent theories, can be described provisionally as vaguely defined "particles" in perpetual motion and that the major portion – i.e. 99.9% – of what we call an "atom" consists of empty space. Nonetheless, according to our shared conventions about reality, physical objects are solid and substantial. And we live in accordance with this belief, notwithstanding the fact that it is still being discussed whether, and if so when, atoms turn into solid mass, that is to say, the physical objects that we are so familiar with in our everyday lives. If we were to encounter a person who states that he or she sees the surrounding reality as it is described in subatomic physics, we might be inclined to say that the person in question is hallucinating!

We also know that the Earth is not flat and we know that it revolves around the sun – and not the other way round. Nevertheless, most of us have no mental or bodily experience of the fact that we live on a ball-shaped planet that is moving at high speed through outer space. Apparently, it runs counter to the ordinary human processing of our sensory perceptions to arrive at any other conclusion than that we move around with our heads extended upward toward the sky and with our feet planted down onto a stationary earth, which appears to be flat and has horizontal extension, as far as the eye can see. And similarly, even though we *know* that the Earth rotates around its own axis, we still experience – and we use, moreover, the figure of speech – that the sun *rises* in the morning and *sets* in the evening. In this respect, our perception of reality is not all that different from the perception of indigenous peoples who have no knowledge of several hundred years of scientific research within the field of astronomy.

It is actually surprising that we do not ask questions that could add to our knowledge and influence our everyday conventional albeit limited perception of reality. Is it possible, for instance, that our notion of reality could be supplemented with experience-based knowledge about phenomena of external reality in the light of the area of validity covered by quantum physics and astrophysics? Or – what would perhaps be just as relevant – in the light of knowledge that could offer us insight into and a sensation of the astonishing fact that reality can be described and perceived as being multidimensional? It could, of course, be argued that in our daily lives, it is both relevant and practical for us to perceive physical objects as solid and for us to apprehend that the sun rises and sets every day, regardless of the fact that there may be other possible ways of perceiving reality.

Knowledge acquired within mathematics and physics is crucial for technological development, which, among other things, constitutes the precondition for developing computer technology applied within the spheres of administration and communication today. Furthermore, new knowledge within astrobiology about the make-up and development of the universe springs from theories and mathematical models that radically break with our conventional way of thinking and perceiving. It may seem strange that this has not caused us to ask questions about whether it is possible – and whether it is desirable – for human beings to experience, and to form concepts and language about, the world and ourselves that are inspired and informed by these current scientific theories and ways of description. [112]

With the study on Mungiki in mind it is thought-provoking that the questions we decide to ask influence not only the knowledge we can acquire but also have an influence to bear on what areas and under what premises we can acquire knowledge. On Mungiki, there clearly were areas that the inhabitants did not feel comfortable about being asked and there clearly were areas which they had not even considered being asked about. The experience of causation, which is so crucial for the understanding of relations and the perception of reality that currently marks Western societies, thus appears to be less dominant in the way that the Mungikis experience the event of reality. [113]

---

[112] Køppe, 1990. Simo Køppe presents, in *Virkelighedens niveauer,* a discussion about Niels Bohr's reflections on knowledge and language and David Bohm's suggestions regarding the formation of a language called "rheomode". This will be elucidated later on in this chapter

[113] Heisenberg, 1986. Werner Heisenberg points out that the conventionally accepted and limiting use of the concept of causality in relation to the law of cause and effect is relatively recent and that this has gained a footing as material processes, along with the development of science in modern times, became more prominent in humanity's perception of reality.

It struck me while staying on the island that Mungikis seem to be more prone than we are to perceiving the presence of everything as a whole, in which the parts form dynamic relations. Like an open field in which the parts present themselves as distinct from other parts and yet, at the same time, are not regarded as separate and isolated. The parts are thus perceived as existing in an organic state of presence in interaction with everything else – interactions that are not necessarily perceived as being causal. If we can assume that this is so, it would then be worth examining whether this implies, moreover, that the Mungikis' perception of reality is determined to a lesser extent than is the Western perception of reality by the perception of space and time of mechanical physics and the related causality thinking. Perhaps the most interesting question in the context of this book is whether the way that the Mungikis experience existence has an influence to bear on their basic perception and attitude to themselves (individually), to each other and to the environment – and hence to their way of life.

The following description of my stay on Mungiki constitutes an attempt to illustrate the conditions of life as well as to conjure up an idea of how the inhabitants of the island meet, shape and live within these conditions.

A different life

To many, a remote palm-encircled island with white beaches arising from the eternally blue Pacific Ocean embodies the dream of Paradise on Earth. But what is it that we are each seeking to fulfill with this notion? And how would we meet the dream if it were to become reality? In the following, I would like to offer an account of my own experiences and considerations.

> *Strong arms helped me off the railing of the ship and down into one of the canoes that carried my luggage and me the last bit of the way onto the white, palm-surrounded beach. From that moment on, I was part of a reality that all at once became my life and existence for an unknown number of months.* [114] *It was as if a postcard came to life. Sounds, colors, smells, and corporeal sensations of people, the lively ripples of the sea, the air, the wind, and the heat in an abundant and kaleidoscopic tropical composition borne forth by the hospitable, helpful and agile Mungikis, men, women and children, who all found their place in the welcoming party. Speaking, laughing, shouting and*

---

114 There was no regular shipping service to the main island of Guadalcanal. Mungiki is situated at the rim of the Solomon Islands, more than a day's travel by ship away from the other islands.

gesticulating, and with attentive care paid to the long-awaited friends and their heavy luggage. After half an hour of walking and climbing up the steep coral cliffs, we came to the village with the hut that was now my home on Mungiki.

Especially in the beginning, it was the fascination with being in the tropics, with its resplendent wealth of colors and strange plants, flowers, animals, and sounds that filled my whole existence. An eagerness to explore the completely different way of life which unfolded in a Polynesian village absorbed me, overwhelmed me and filled me with a mixture of deep excitement, wonder and astonishment. The experience of intense and saturated presence alternated at times with a feeling of un-realness. As if I needed to make sure that what I was experiencing was not a dream that I could wake up from any minute.

In the course of time, it all became daily life and I was part of the rhythm of the small community, where everyday activities and doings are adapted to the sun, the nature and the shifting weather. Where everything that is created, made and produced for the sustenance of life is done with simple tools and the bare hands' and agile bodies' unerring movements on land, at sea, and in the high palms that provide fruits and coconuts, which are, in turn, an important source of water. The unwavering way life evolves in a place on Earth where the technological developments of the modern age and the market have not yet arrived and where everybody cooperates and shares the crops and the catches among themselves. Where precisely this order of society ensures the life and survival of everybody.

In a matter of a few days, I, much like the few other researchers who had earlier obtained permission to stay on the island, had to realize my deep dependence on the Mungikis. The knowledge and prowess of the Mungikis enable them to cultivate the scarce soil and bring forth, gather and process the crops that provide food for everybody. Although this is accomplished with extremely primitive methods of production, it ensures the most efficient yield and prevents the depletion of the soil and the natural vegetation.

Sofus Christiansen, an internationally renowned Danish professor in cultural geography and a pioneer in the development of sustainable organic farming, tried to introduce spades and other slightly more advanced tools of cultivation during his stay on Mungiki as replacements for the Mungikis' use of their fingers and digging-sticks when planting and collecting crops. Furthermore, he tried to systematize and order the plots in order to make them more manageable. After some months, he had to realize that the varied character and suitability of the soil for the rich variation of plants as well as the Mungikis' special sensitivity toward and considerable knowledge about all this were crucial preconditions for their being able to provide for themselves. It even turned out that the mode of cultivation made Mungiki farming one of the most efficient procedures going on in the world, when measured in calories invested relative to the calories of the yield. [115]

What seemed remarkable to me was the degree to which the Mungikis were at one with their natural surroundings. Their life unfolds in activities of planting and gathering crops, in activities of finding and adjusting suitable logs, branches, plants and bark for making huts, sleeping mats, canoes and tools, and in activities of collecting rocks, twigs, and palm leaves for preparing the daily meals of vegetables and fish to be backed in the earth ovens – the center around which the life of the family evolves.

On Mungiki, you are not in a hurry. Everything takes place in a calm rhythm, from the moment that you get up at dawn and begin the doings of the day. There's always time to stop and talk to someone who comes by and tells stories. The young people especially sit down from time to time in small packs and sing Polynesian songs, accompanied by ukuleles. Both men and women take time to stop on their way to and from their daily chores and adorn themselves with the colorful flowers of the hibiscus trees. Or they sit in small groups, weaving sleeping mats and bags in classical Polynesian patterns while looking after children of all ages who are running around and playing. If you need to take a rest, you lie down for a quick nap, whether you are in your own hut, happen to be visiting others or are just in the middle of activities with others.

Soon I was engulfed in carrying out my fieldwork and absorbed in the preparation of collecting data. It was not until several weeks of work had passed and after having started the interviews I was conducting with families in all three districts on the island that I could relax a little. It was at that point that I discovered, on my way home from an interview I had made at the other end of the island that I was no longer walking on the main path through the tropical forest as though I was on a brisk walk in a Danish beech forest. Up until then, the speed at which I walked had made it necessary for me to take

---
115 Christiansen, 1975

several pauses on the way so that my interpreter and any others who had joined company with us could catch up with me. I now realized that it was me who had been "caught up" with them – not because the Mungikis were turning up their pace but rather by my adjusting to their peaceful, agile, and light rhythm and to their attentive way of being present, regardless of where they were. I felt a calm that I had not known before and I noticed that my thought activity had imperceptibly subsided and that I was concerned exclusively with the time and space of the moment in which I found myself. Overtaken by a sensorial experience of the place and of myself as the epitome of the simultaneity of everything – as a whole, in which everything is in dynamic interaction and expression and in which sense perceptions merge and amplify one another in an experience of reality that is inseparable from reality itself.

It was the first time since my childhood that I experienced being thrilled by a sense of joy and gratitude that occurs in a golden moment in which presence is freed from concepts that affirm the divides between everything in existence and where existence itself seems to hold you – caress you.

I do not mean to claim that I understood the Mungikis better from this point on. Nor did I suddenly have a better understanding of the apparently inexplicable incidences that I experienced time and time again– but perhaps these things didn't astonish me as much anymore. For instance, there was one morning when the clouds were hanging heavy and low and I showed my interpreter that I had remembered my umbrella, and I was met with a dry retort that it would not be needed. And, well, only moments later, it was brilliant sunshine – that lasted for the rest of the day. And, then again, on the other hand, there was also the time that I, on one lovely sunny morning, was reminded to remember my umbrella. A short while later, having heeded this advice saved me from being drenched by an hour-long tropical shower. And there was the time when I, minutes after having cleansed and dressed the deep wound of a young man who had been caught in the arm by a swordfish, spotted his family arriving at my village from the other end of the island some ten kilometers away. My repeated questions, asking them how they knew he had been hurt and how they – only an hour after he had been injured – could cover the considerable distance through the pitch-black night in the tropical forest, quite literally in no time, were met with nothing but a shrug.

No explanation was needed.

It was not until I had returned home and had started to examine and reflect on the results of my field study that it started to dawn on me how the Mungikis' experience of reality is shaping their way of life. It occurred to me that their sense of being deeply connected to each other, to nature, to the weather and to the seasons is a precondition for their way of perception and their way of living in respect and care for each other and in harmony with their natural surroundings. I also reflected on the fact that everyone helps everybody else and that the crops and catches are shared among them. Owning a lot of land and having the largest canoes simply means that you have more to give. Generosity, considerateness and composure are among the most highly valued qualities on Mungiki. This does not mean to say that the Mungikis always live up to these values. On the contrary, they believe that envy and slander are among their most common flaws and the most common causes of the recurring conflicts, of which the islanders are deeply ashamed. Nonetheless, it is precisely the ability to be generous and considerate toward others that is so highly revered and that was most frequently expressed among the Mungikis: these are personality traits that give prestige and which characterize the informal leaders among them.

A state of aware presence combined with the experience of calm, joy, and carefree connectedness with everything in existence is perhaps the closest we can come to the notion of Elysian life on a Pacific island. It was not at all as steady a state of mind for me as it seemed to be for the Mungikis. It almost came and went, depending on the force of my habitual thoughts and feelings, apprehensions and hopes, worries, aggravations, bouts of self-interest and demands on myself for results and achievements – especially in connection with making my field study. But I realized that it was at those times when my consciousness and the flow of my thoughts fell silent and I became present in the natural union of everything that the really significant insights, discoveries and realizations about everything under the sun emerged – completely effortlessly, as if out of thin air.[116]

---

[116] Penrose, 1994. The physicist, Roger Penrose, has said that his best work did not spring from a deductive logical process but from sudden intuitions and insights into an indescribably beautiful Platonic realm. Penrose's statement expresses an experience that not only prominent scientists and creative artists throughout history have told about. This also occurs in daily life when we, for example, gain an insight or see the solution to a problem while brushing our teeth in the morning or waiting at the bus stop – or we when, for one time's sake, sit around just looking straight in front of us without thinking of anything in particular.

Glimpses of change

Mungiki is not a paradise on Earth and perhaps we can make do with less. For as sunny, lush, and immensely beautiful as life may be there, it can be equally harsh. The Mungikis are, for example, completely dependent on the tropical weather where hot sun shining from an endless blue sky vacillates between extremes of drought and periods where tropical storms ravage – with rain, wind and bolts of lightning, the latter threatening to sweep the huts and crops away and chop off the tops of the coconut palms. And because the weather sometimes prevents fishing from the slender canoes, the Mungikis can hardly keep hunger at bay. But it is as if they live flexibly with the variability of the times and meet the changing conditions with an innate ability to appraise them and meet them and with a pragmatic approach.

As a Westerner for whom easy access to an abundant variety of foods, comforts, consumer goods, electricity and water is taken for granted and who is used to being able to communicate with the environment, you have to relinquish all this for as long as your stay on the island lasts. Having access to transportation and being confident that you can get to and get back from a place, whenever you need to do so – for example, in cases of serious illness – must also be given up. The reward is that you discover aspects of yourself, others, the natural surroundings and life in its entirety, which in itself is deeply enriching.

It is with a mixture of the genuine sadness at having to leave and the happy expectations of resuming life at home that you, on the day of departure, walk to the beach for the last time. And as you see the island disappear in the horizon from the stern of the ship, there's no doubt that you are not really who you used to be anymore. The wish to preserve the contact with the peace and the newly discovered depths inside yourself is still vitally present, especially in the hours and days immediately following your departure. And it remains a strong impulse until you allow the life at home to overwhelm you once again, with the cacophonic and noisy sense-bombardment and high-speed rush of the city, the fast communication, the busy people and all the commitments, performance demands and expectations, as well as the surfeit of available goods of any kind that are difficult to relate to and choose between. The wish to retain the atmosphere, the rhythm, and the insights about life that were part and parcel of the time spent on Mungiki is apparently drowned out by the relentless pulse of civilization and becomes suppressed by a conflicting urge to follow familiar patterns that give you a peculiar sense of comfort. Because they stand as a reassurance that your identity is intact. With astonishing speed, *you're back!* – Almost as if nothing had happened.

It was, however, as if a chord had been struck, the resonance of which changed my basic mood and influenced my attitude in various situations. For instance, when I was subject to especially strenuous situations on Mungiki – like when my leg was sliced open by lethal coral or when the ship carrying me from Mungiki to Honiara was hit by a tropical hurricane – and I, in both of these cases, found myself surrendering to the situation in the calm acceptance that I might not survive. Even if my new basic mood did not lead to what could be described as an overwhelming transformation of my life, I noticed that once I was back home, I no longer felt a sense of restlessness and annoyance at queuing up or waiting for a delayed bus. It was as if I had invariably adapted myself to being present in the special rhythm of the situation, which I share with the others standing in the line.

The same, yet incomparable

Paradoxically enough, it was already clear from the outset that the Mungikis, basically and altogether recognizably, are human beings who are very much like us. At the same time, there also are certain modes of being in the world that make us incomparable. Perhaps the motto, "unity in diversity", is appropriate here. This insight completely altered – as has been mentioned – the focus of my field study. From my initially being concerned with conducting a comparative statistical survey of the differences in parameters pertaining to the socialization of aggression in the West and on Mungiki, it became more meaningful for me to show that it is sometimes fruitless to subject human differences to (quantitative) comparison. And this is so partly because we risk making faulty observations and conclusions and partly because we miss out on valuable knowledge.

The natural conditions of life on Mungiki are clearly different from ours. Yet it would nonetheless be tantamount to making an oversimplification to argue that the Mungikis are different from us strictly because of their having to perceive reality differently in order to live a life according to their actual basic conditions. Such an argument fails to take into account that we, as human beings, are not merely controlled by our surroundings. It is rather with a point of departure taken in our basic values and our view of humanity, as reflected in our perceptions and attitudes, that we, in mutual interaction with the surroundings, actively create, shape and contribute to our basis of existence and concrete reality. It is here that we find the crux of the difference between the Mungikis and ourselves: it is obvious that the Mungikis, for generations, have been able to live in harmony with and respect for the rather limited natural resources and it is obvious that they have been able to sustain themselves. They have, moreover, practiced cooperation in the production as well as in the distribution of vital necessities.

Nothing has prevented us in the Western civilization from handling our circumstances and leading our lives based on the same values, motives, and insights as those held by the Mungikis. However, it does seem that we in the Western World have believed for a good many centuries that we could set aside considerations of our basic motives and values. That we, as a consequence of "progress thinking" and spurred on by the vision of technological and economic superiority, have let ourselves be allured by novel possibilities for growth and wealth. This abstention, which has occurred at the expense of the experience of connectedness and at the expense of respect for the natural surroundings and our fellow human beings has increasingly made it possible to build and expand affluent societies – for a minority of the population on Earth. And we doggedly continue to do this, notwithstanding that we have known full well for many years that our common survival is thereby being threatened and that we are about to cross over the line demarcating the end of our continued existence on this planet.

It is strange that we can keep on upholding the notion of the superiority of our own civilization over earlier and currently different forms of society and cultures. And furthermore, it is strange that we find this position to be legitimized by the power that our economic superiority ensures us. It is no less paradoxical that the technological and scientific conquests, which we believe to be a testimony to a higher degree of intelligence, knowledge, breadth of view, innovative thinking and human capability, have not prompted us to carefully consider whether our innovations are actually beneficial and not harmful.

An indigenous people like the inhabitants of Mungiki - along with other indigenous peoples -represents an invaluable testimony to us because these populations show us that it is humanly possible to create a life that, even if it is far from being perfect and Elysian, still rests on an ethical foundation and on empathy that not only ensures people's survival but also a life in which human beings and their natural surroundings are part of an equal interaction within the totality that constitutes the existence of all there is.

CHAPTER 7
LANGUAGE AND THE MULTIFACETED REALITY

With reference to the language and the perception of reality on the Polynesian island of Mungiki, and in other non-Western cultures, it seems likely that people in some parts of the world, due to respective differences in their historical and cultural conditions, experience dimensions of reality that are simply unknown to us or dimensions that we are simply not aware of in our part of the world. Furthermore, their language appears to accommodate the communication of such experiences of reality. This might serve, in turn, to reinforce the capacity to experience these other levels of reality. What is discussed here is whether this promotes living in harmony with – and in respect for – nature and whether it promotes respect for equal access to – and the sharing of – the means of sustenance. As an illustration of this the chapter concludes with a personal testimony from life on Mungiki.

Language, identity and the all-encompassing reality

In the previous chapter, the question was raised about whether the Mungikis' perception of reality is determined to a lesser degree than ours by the perception of space and time espoused by mechanistic physics and the closely related causality. The description of the Mungikis' perception of reality and way of life as it appears from the outside renders this probable. Apparently, this is furthermore reflected in their language, since there are no subjects and objects connected to the verbs. The subject, for instance, is not indicated in the sentence structure but is rather shown indirectly by the use of verbs. The personal pronoun, "I", does not exist in the language. The absence of subject and object designations in the language could serve to indicate that the Mungikis do not maintain a clear distinction between subject and object, that is to say, they do not necessarily operate with a clear-cut subject-object duality. The use of verbs to express being, states, relations, and dynamic processes transpiring between non-explicitly specified subjects and objects could serve to indicate that their perception of reality is characterized by a lesser degree of fixation on an "I" as an isolated identity. It is accordingly probable that the Mungikis are more inclined than we are to experience existence as a state of unity in a spontaneously arising flow of mutual interaction.

Whether such a perception of reality, which is not necessarily reserved exclusively for indigenous peoples like the Mungikis, could be developed in our own culture and could thereby contribute to a lessening of the growing isolation and fragmentation on both the individual and societal level is worth considering. As we touched upon earlier, it could be interesting to examine whether the formation of language and concepts about the world and ourselves that are inspired and informed by our current scientific theories and descriptions within, for instance, quantum mechanics, could contribute to this.

It was precisely reflections like these that one of the most prominent physicists of the previous century, David Bohm, set out to investigate. [117] Like many other outstanding researchers within the sciences, he devoted his life to developing scientific studies of phenomena in the physical world while simultaneously contemplating and seeking to invent methods to apprehend the nature of existence beyond the reality of the physical world. Bohm was – like many other brilliant researchers – concerned with the philosophical, ethical, and practical implications of scientific research and of the technological developments of his day. He was especially concerned with the ever-growing imbalance he noticed in humanity's relation to nature as well as in relations between people. Bohm was thus deeply worried about what was happening to humanity at a time when technology was roaring ahead with increasing force – and as he noticed: either at the service of good or of destruction.

In his book, *Wholeness and the Implicate Order*, Bohm spoke out against, among others, Niels Bohr and the Copenhagen school. [118] One of the main assumptions of the Copenhagen school is that language, in its conceptual structure and semantics, presupposes the core notions of mechanical physics, i.e., causality, determination, space and time, and the separation between subject and object. Both Bohm and Albert Einstein disagreed with Bohr insofar as they rejected the idea of a built-in mechanical semantics of language, which implies that we cannot consciously perceive and comprehend phenomena which transcend the mechanical static and ahistorical language barrier of mechanical semantics. [119] To this could be added, that in order to transcend the limitation

---
117 Keepin, 1993
118 Bohm, 1980
119 Køppe, 1990

of our conventional language and ordinary minds reasoning we have to develop our capacity to directly experiencing reality beyond the dimension of mechanical physics.

Bohm develops what he calls a "rheomode" on the basis of linguistic studies, in which nouns are transformed into verbs. The point was to change our perception of phenomena and objects as delimited and static entities and instead make room for a notion of reality in which objects are dynamic entities, unfolding in space and time. Thereby, a linguistic formulation of reality as processes in dynamic and perpetual unfolding within an indivisible universal field is achieved, in which everything is inseparable from the totality.

It is thought-provoking that Bohm's reflections on the emancipation of conventional language and its capacity to facilitate experiences of another order than that which has been determined by classical mechanics seem to have traits in common with, for instance, the Mungikis' language and perception of reality. [120] Bohm observed, on the basis of historical studies within philosophy and epistemology that the way we perceive phenomena and reality is in a mutual dependent relation with our thinking. He discovered that we, earlier on in human history, did not always perceive the parts or entities as isolated and independent of the totality – in the way we are now prone to doing.

Bohm perceived the sources of the challenges that we are meeting now to be the very way we think and our attempts to solve problems with the same kind of thinking that created the problems. This can be likened, he noted, to going to visit the doctor and having him make us sick. Bohm was incessantly engaged in efforts to prepare the ground for the realization of his vision for a complete restructuring of our fragmented collective consciousness and he was hoping to pave the way for the advent of a new renaissance. [121] He was convinced about the necessity of a movement similar to the one created during the Renaissance, only an even deeper and more comprehensive one, so that rigid intellectual and mental structures in consciousness could be dissolved and the "hardness of the heart" could melt. It was Bohm's wish that a dissolution of habitual thought patterns and fixed mental structures could awaken a truly creative intelligence and that an emotional softening of mind and hearts could be the forerunner for real love among human beings and life on Earth. For Bohm, creative intelligence and love were inseparably connected.

---
120 Something similar is, e.g., the case with the original Tibetan written language.
121 Bohm & Peat, 1987

Reflections on language

In the following, we will examine whether it is *language itself* that limits our ability to experience different aspects and levels of reality or whether it *our assumptions about language and our ways of relating to language* that create obstacles to our experience of reality.

If we assume that our common language has an inherent semantics that corresponds to a specific level of description of reality, for instance, to the level of reality of mechanistic physics, we will invariably be confronted by insurmountable obstacles when we attempt to acquire knowledge and when we attempt to communicate about levels of reality that apparently unfold completely differently. If we uphold the thesis that these levels of reality can only be described according to the common language if they are to be communicated at all then we are confronted with serious impediments when it comes to communicate about the levels of the reality of quantum mechanics. [122] Knowledge about reality, which is thus bound to language and determined by language use, will invariably be locked inside the narrow space of the possibilities of the particular language.

One very simple example can refute the assumptions 1) that everything that can be known can be communicated linguistically and 2) that whatever is experienced and known that cannot be communicated linguistically cannot be ascribed valid existence. Anyone who has tasted an avocado has no doubt that its taste can be experienced and that this flavor is unique and different from other taste experiences. It is, however, not possible to describe the taste of avocado by means of verbal communication. And it is especially difficult to communicate this special taste experience to someone who has never tasted this particular fruit. However, people who know the taste of avocado will be able to speak about variations in the taste of avocados and they will be able to point out and express agreement about whether an avocado is unripe, ripe or overripe. This communication is considered to be about a phenomenon – taste – that is conventionally ascribed valid existence even if we cannot prove whether two different people have the very same taste experiences.

Human beings are unique in using highly complex languages. It seems obvious that there is a difference between languages and language use due to i.e. environmental and social conditions in different cultures and

---

[122] Without pretending to have a deeper understanding of quantum mechanics and without claiming to have any special insight into the philosophical argument of the Copenhagen school, it seems reasonable to assume that Bohr sought to overcome this paradox by introducing the principle of complementarity. Supposedly, precisely the problem of communication was, for Bohr, a never-finished project.

that difference in language and the use of language express different perceptions of reality.

Perhaps we could make the general assumption that what humans have in common is that they experience reality, to a greater or lesser extent, in the way it is described and unfolds within the framework of mechanical physics: that they generally experience physical phenomena as solid objects; that they are subject to what we call gravity; that subjects and objects are separate and independent entities; and that everything unfolds in space and time in the form of causal relations. However, it seems that people in *some* parts in the world, because of differences in historical and cultural conditions, experience levels of reality that in our part of the world are unknown to us or that we do not notice. Furthermore, their languages appear to be formed in a way that not only makes it possible to communicate such experiences of reality but also reinforces experiencing these levels of reality.

The language of the Mungikis evidently makes it possible for these island dwellers to operate linguistically within alternating levels of reality. This does not necessarily entail that they are deprived of the possibility of also experiencing the level of reality of mechanical physics. Both levels of reality are part of their consciousness and experience – perhaps in the sense that they can alternate spontaneously between these two levels of reality according to the situation they experience being in. On the basis of this assumption, it makes sense that the Mungiki occasionally will give causal explanations for what occurs and occasionally not.

Bohm stands as one of countless examples that even people in our own culture – using languages that supposedly constitute a barrier to experiences of reality that lie beyond the level of reality of mechanical physics – nonetheless experience reality beyond this level. Furthermore, he was able to communicate his experience. In an interview conducted just a few years before his death, Bohm – who in his adult years was an agnostic – related that he, in his childhood, had experienced reality as an undivided totality akin to the reality about which he later on, as a physicist, tried to construct a large-scale theory. [123] This experience of being as undivided totality happened when he, with his Jewish family, recited a special daily prayer in Hebrew about loving God with all your heart, soul and mind. The experience of totality was not decidedly aimed at God but rather expressed a way of being in life that came to be crucial for him. Likewise, he experienced, early on in his life, the feeling that he and nature were a unity and he felt a deep inner connection with the

---
123 Bohm & Peat, 1987

trees, the mountains and the stars. These experiences and realizations are, it goes without saying, recognizable to many people in our own and other cultures. But what is interesting in Bohm's case is that he, during his studies of quantum physics, spontaneously had the same experience of undivided totality in dynamic unfolding. Bohm, in his own words, experienced the reality of quantum physics directly: it was not just a matter of constructs that he thought up.

For Bohm, there was no contradiction between the description of reality within highly advanced scientific explorations of the phenomena of the physical world and, for instance, his own and indigenous people's experience of reality as a union with nature and everything that unfolds in our existence. According to Bohm, this awareness and this way of knowing have deep implications on the ethical basis of life for humanity and on our ways of relating to each other and the natural surroundings. It was therefore important to Bohm to find a way – a language – that could not only express this but also make it possible for people to develop this form of experience of realty.

We might ask, then, whether it is necessary, as Bohm believed, to develop a special language in order to experience and communicate such a reality. Or whether we can use the language that we already have if we actually keep in mind that language is a way of communicating about reality but not a necessary condition for knowing and experiencing reality. Language is undoubtedly extremely important but it is not the only tool to make oneself understood in communication between people. From this point of view, language does not in itself constitute the experience of reality. Moreover, language cannot mediate a comprehensive representation of reality and the experience hereof. We can find proof of this in the experiences that most ordinary language users have had, namely, that it's not everything we know and that appears clearly and undeniably which can be formulated and communicated linguistically. [124]

Our fundamental ability to perceive and learn from others who are not like ourselves is probably an upshot of our urge to explore, an urge that is based on the wish to understand ourselves and the other, an urge that is not always dependent on what language we use. Deeper mutual

---

[124] Lakoff and Johnson, 1999. According to linguist George Lakoff, we experience the world through our bodies and sense faculties, and this way of seeing the world has, in the course of time, become sedimented in our languages. The metaphors we form linguistically thus mirror bodily sensations. Lakoff's theory builds on the assumption of an intimate, "non-dualistic" relation between body and mind, expressed in the concept: "the embodied mind".

understanding often applies levels of awareness and consciousness that are open to realization beyond language, time, and history.

Questions we refrain from asking

In common with the islanders on Mungiki, we also have ignorance, although it is apparently not the same areas about which we are cognizant and ignorant. It is also not necessarily the same areas that we find it relevant and interesting to acquire knowledge about. There is, however, one point at which we seem to differ crucially from the Mungikis: we consciously choose to abstain from acquiring knowledge about certain areas of reality. These abstentions imply that we are consciously refraining from knowing about selected areas of human life and existence.

Even though the natural sciences have brought the concepts of objectivity, subjectivity and causality into completely new frames of understanding and have pointed toward the existence of manifold dimensions of reality, we abstain, for instance, from acquiring basic knowledge about human consciousness and about the very levels of consciousness that constitute a precondition to operating with and devising theories about the multidimensionality of the physical world. It is thus a widespread assumption that it is the brain that takes care of thinking and that it is only possible to explore consciousness scientifically in connection with brain studies performed by neuroscience research. Furthermore, it is assumed that consciousness cannot explore itself. What remains unclear is whether the brain can explore itself and whether it is the brain that tells the neuroscientist that it wants to be explored. We could say that abstaining from a comprehensive scientific study of consciousness appears to be a conscious choice of ignorance. [125]

Ignorance is thus not solely – as we might be led to believe from Edmund Leach's argument – a question of lacking skills in logical and rational argumentation. It is also a matter of questions that we refrain from asking and areas that we consciously abstain from dealing with.

We might ask ourselves whether it meant that much to the Mungikis that they did not know about the relation between intercourse and pregnancy. Life went on – and the women got the children they wanted. In cases of infertility, by which many couples on Mungiki were afflicted, it was a widespread practice that families with many children would simply let the childless couple adopt one of their own.

---

[125] Buddhist philosophy and contemplative method point to the exploration and training of consciousness that uphold the common rules of science, such as logically consistent argumentation, controlled methods of research and empirical validation.

What we can learn from Mungiki

In the Buddhist cultures in Asia – which, like the Mungikis, have developed languages that reflect other levels of perception of reality – the individual will to a higher degree be seen in the light of her/his relationship to the community. There is a tendency in the West to view this as an expression of the individual's being subordinate to the totality, in the sense of being less significant than the community. The life of the individual is thus alleged to be less important in these cultures than in our own. This is a clear example of ethnocentrism, which only testifies to a lack of experience with the fact that everything that is part of the totality is equal to and inseparable from the totality, which is neither more nor less significant than the constituent individual parts. This does not mean that everyone who is part of the totality is identical and the same. Every individual is characterized by his or her specific appearance, by his or her specific qualities and can be known and valued for the way the person expresses these.

The difference between what's going on in our part of the world and other parts of the world in which individualism is not so prevalent as it is with us, is probably that people there will be less prone to engaging in self-absorption and self-interest that comes from being alien to one's authentic qualities and ways of unfolding them in mutual relations with others.

It cannot be proven that the Mungiki perception of reality embodies levels of consciousness that further considerate conduct toward each other and the surrounding nature. But it is beyond the shadow of a doubt that they, for as long as they have been inhabitants of Mungiki, have lived in harmony with and respect for nature and with a consensus about supporting equal access to the means of sustenance, and it is beyond debate that this has been a precondition of these people's survival. It is also indisputable that they value human qualities like generosity, composure and considerateness, notwithstanding that, to their own regret, it is far from always that they are able to fully live up to these virtues. It is, however, these traits that characterize their informal leaders who, no matter how much they own, are willing to share with others and who remain even-tempered, friendly and sober-minded and also refrain from aggressive outbursts, engaging in slander, or perpetrating other actions that would cause strife.

It would be invaluable if we, in our part of the world, could assign the same qualities and ethical attitudes to the people we choose to entrust as our leaders and who we, through democratic elections, give the power to represent us and to lead our nations.

Communal sharing and caring

In a most concrete way, I experienced the generosity and caring that was part of communal life on Mungiki: it was actually a precondition for my survival on the island. An economy based on the exchange of money did not exist and I, time and again, had to contain myself and abstain from immediately giving something in exchange when I was offered food. Or from wanting to "pay back" with rice, sugar or pencils when somebody did me a favor. This would have been considered highly improper and would have deprived the Mungikis of their joy in being generous.

The Mungikis were very well aware of – and more than I was myself – how much I needed them. There were no natural sources of drinking water on the island. Potable water was accessed by gathering rainwater. However, due to periods of drought, the most reliable sources for quelling the thirst were the not-fully-ripe coconuts that were still hanging high up in the palms. Only boys and young men were able to climb up to get them. Imperceptibly, a fresh supply was brought to my hut whenever it was needed.

It was, however, not only the physical necessities that were taken care of. During the first week of my stay, my hut was the hangout where Mungikis gathered all day long – observing with great interest every step I took. One morning as I woke up and, as usual, stared directly into the eyes of a number of Mungikis gathered around my bed, I just had it. Sick and tired of what I considered these people's totally shameless curiosity I, making large gesticulations and loud sounds, chased them away in order to regain privacy for at least the breadth of my precious, peaceful morning hours, in my own company. After this incident and for the rest of my stay, the Mungikis gathered instead under my hut and I woke up in the early mornings to the sound of their chatting together and singing Polynesian songs.

It was not until much later that I, while making an interview, realized that the Mungikis, out of sheer concern for me, were making sure that I was not alone. Knowing full well that I had been traveling so very far from home and that I was so far away from my community, and for such a long time, they assumed that what I really needed was that they would be there for me and would care for me. And they wanted to make sure that I was not missing my dear ones at home all too much.

It was not the first time that I quietly felt ashamed of my lack of consideration for the Mungikis and their way of thinking and behaving. I also, to my deep regret, violated their norms and rules many times without knowing that I was doing so. It was especially at the beginning of my stay that I had a hard time concealing my impatience and irritation with them. The Mungikis, for their part, never made any remarks about my transgressions of their norms. For example, when I, in my insatiable craving for understanding the Mungikis, bombarded them with all kinds of questions that, according to their customs, were not altogether proper to ask.

The fact that the Mungikis did not make any remarks about my transgressions did not mean that they weren't noticing them. Their way of relating to all my many questions and to my demands for explanations at all times – and their response to the fact that I could not comprehend that things just happen – was to give me the nickname: Etia. Etia means: "she who asks why".

Taupongi's journey

To bring my reflections of my meeting with the culture on Mungiki to a conclusion, I would like to give the floor to one of the inhabitants of the island, a man going by the name of Taupongi. The following account can be interpreted as a comment by Taupongi on his encounter with our culture.

Taupongi was an informant in a class of his own, with enormous knowledge about the history of the island and its religion, as well as its customs, its social structures and the agriculture and fishing activities. He was invited to come to Denmark by Professor Torben Monberg to support the work of clarifying data collected by Danish researchers who had visited Mungiki.

The researchers were curious to learn how Taupongi would manage the transition from the primitive conditions of his island and how he would cope with living in our highly developed world for some months.

Taupongi seemed to be completely comfortable with what he encountered. It was almost as if he merely took note that matters were just as he had been told in advance. It was natural for him to respect the different customs in our culture and he took notice of them without questioning them.

At one point, Taupongi ran up against a barrier. It was not that he was unwilling to accept what he had witnessed. But he simply could not fathom what was going on. It occurred during his first train ride to the home of the researcher he was living with. What met Taupongi – and what was incomprehensible to him – is something that we consider to be altogether commonplace and natural.

When he was about to recount his experience, he laughed long and heartily. It took him several minutes, interrupted by repeated fits of laughter, to tell the family what was so hilarious. In the moments in which he composed himself, he related how he walked into the train compartment and saw that people were sitting like pillars of stone, looking out into thin air or maybe reading a newspaper, as if they were not aware or taking any notice of the fact that they were on a train ride and about what was taking place around them. And even more curiously: they never greeted or spoke to each other, for instance, about the purpose of their journey – or were they were going.

At first, the sight that met him dumbfounded Taupongi. But all at once, the whole scenery seemed so absurd and hilarious that he burst out into a high and roaring laughter. And between his renewed bursts of laughter, he told the wondering family that he was laughing and laughing during the whole ride. And he kept laughing and laughing - until tears ran down his cheeks...

CHAPTER 8
SEEING THE EXTRAORDINARY IN THE ORDINARY

The experience of the real, the true nature of existence, which – in a flash – illuminates us from within, is among the most precious and most genuine moments in our lives. It is therefore remarkable that most of the time we live in a state of unconsciousness, dissociated from our true being, as if this mode of living were the most natural thing in the world. It is precisely this question that has always – and in all cultures – concerned humanity. The experience of the sublime, the extraordinary, which elates and moves us in the one moment, only to be superseded in the next moment by the everyday, humdrum and drab perception of reality, has been, for some people, the impetus for a deep sense of wonder – and, for others, a cause for deep longing. It is this wonder and longing that have been basic motives for exploring and for reflecting on the truth about humanity, its origin, expression, and reality formation.

With the "ethical paradox": "For I don't do the good I want; instead, the evil that I don't want is what I do" - as a point of departure it is established that – whether we adhere to an existential or a biological perspective of the nature of man – it is possible for human beings to distinguish, to make choices, and to act on the basis of intelligent judgment, empathy and compassion. It is indeed possible, if we step out of ignorance and a stance of denial about who we are and what we are actually capable of as human beings.

Dream and reality

> *I am dreaming. I am in an intensive care unit. I am alone – and obviously dying. On monitors, I can follow how one organ after another slowly gives out. I am not afraid of dying but I am a little worried at the thought about the very moment of death – the moment at which after an exhalation, no inhalation will follow. I am sure that it is only moments away. Suddenly, it is as if the countdown is halted, the monitors show stability, and I note that I apparently still have some time*

left. In the next second, a silence beyond all silence occurs. In a flash, I see a brilliant light so clear and strong, as if from a thousand stars, and I feel the light's boundless space of love and wisdom engulfing me. In my complete joy at leaving everything behind me, I walk into the ocean of light and become one with infinite truth.

In the next moment, I found myself lying in my bed. It was early in the morning. My first impulse was a sense of deep regret at having been torn out of a reality infinitely true and more brilliant, clearer, and more loving than the pale reflection of the reality I was slowly waking up to. However, the experience was so intense, filling every cell in my body – and it continued to do so in the following days and weeks.

My disappointment at being alive in my physical body was replaced by a deep sense of gratitude for having experienced once more a glimpse of the all-encompassing truth, wisdom, and boundless goodness of true being. The truth that I, in that moment, realized as being the origin of and inseparably present in everything – regardless of whether we call it life or death and regardless of whether we are conscious of it or not. And I felt an almost irresistible urge to put my dressing gown on and walk to the streets and tell everyone I met that they never again have to fear death and that life in reality holds everything we can wish for.

I came to terms with the thought. But I decided to call my mother and tell her about my dream later in the morning at a time when I knew she would be having her breakfast. It is actually extremely rare for me to talk to others about experiences like this – let alone anybody in my family. But I thought that my dream could be helpful to her. She was well into her seventies and, in my view, she had to have one foot in the grave at that age – and fear the worst.

My mother listened in silence to my account about the dream and its uplifting message. After a while, she broke her silence. She said that at the moment I had called, she was actually reading some advertising material sent from a supermarket and that if I was interested, I could get three packs of ground beef at half price.

My mother reached the ripe age of 96. I never succeeded in touching on this subject again with her, even though I tried several times over the years. Before she died, it had become less taboo to talk about death and to talk about what you thought about death. It was recommended that relatives should engage in this difficult conversation and unveil the solitude of the dying person and share whatever you believed was at the heart of the matter. My mother listened patiently to any attempts I made along these lines. It was, however, more suitable for her to want to talk about her preferred media darling on the late news on television and about what he had said or done so cleverly. And about that nice young doctor from Pakistan – and Member of Parliament – who had inspired her to cast her vote for the Socialist People's Party.

For her part, my mother tried over the years to talk me into going to concerts and art shows and into reading current literature. These pursuits meant the world to her and she was engaged in doing these kinds of things with some of her friends. Actually, I thought that her preoccupation with art was mixed with a certain snobbishness and a wish to belong to the upper rungs of society.

After her death, I came to think of a conversation I had with her when she was 92 and I realized how wrong I had been. It happened when she told me that she had shortly before traveled, all by herself, by bus – bringing a lunchbox – to The Royal Theatre in Copenhagen to hear an opera cycle that lasted all day – and over the course of several days. Remembering the conversation made me understand that art, to her, was the entrance into a reality that was inexpressible and elevated above everything that human beings can fathom. That she, in the course of those days she spent at the opera, unconditionally surrendered to the enormous space of euphony, beauty and lofty human and existential drama. That, seated there in the darkness, she became one with the operatic work of art, the musicians, the singers and the unknown listeners sitting in the rows of seats around her. When she told me about what for her was like setting out on a pilgrimage and about her experience of being freed and cleansed to the core of her soul, her eyes glowed knowingly and with a brilliant light that I had only rarely had the opportunity to witness.

The imperceptible self-forgetfulness
Most of us have experienced extraordinary moments of presence in self-forgetting union with everything in existence – with another person, with nature or a piece of art – and we have realized, in that instant, the inexpressible goodness and infinite beauty of being. Such a moment can be so intensely real and enriching that we stop in pensiveness and rest in the reverberations, filled by sensations of joy and gratitude for the inexplicable moment. Moments of self-forgetting presence are actually not as rare as we are inclined to believe. Perhaps we do not notice

them because they are so mundane and natural. And because they are so fleeting.

Moments of self-forgetting presence in the pure space of awareness occur in the milliseconds between one thought that ends and a new one that arises. A space of awareness in which we directly perceive and sense what is. When we, for instance, in open aware presence, meet another, in fleeting eye contact, or when we perceive the beauty of a flower, when we get an insight, or when we spontaneously know what is needed and without further ado act according to this hunch. It is in these moments that we, being present in our natural state, know what is beneficial to ourselves and others – without ulterior motives or agendas – and without having to think any more about it, we act accordingly. In this aware presence, the giver and the receiver imperceptibly become one in mutual exchange.

It is in the self-forgetting, attentive presence that the inner estrangement is dissolved and we are closest to ourselves. (The one) I am is experienced more real in its fullness and yet as being light and transparent – freed from the veils of concepts and preconceived opinions. According to Buddhist philosophy and understanding of existence, we experience, in these moments, the natural state of mind and existence.

The unification of supposedly irreconcilable aspects

Our experiences of the real, the true nature of existence that – in a flash – illuminates from within, are the most precious and most genuine moments in our lives. It is therefore remarkable that we, most of the time, live in unconsciousness, apart from our true being, as if it were the most natural thing in the world to do so.

It is exactly this question that has always, and in all cultures, concerned humanity. The experience of the sublime, the extraordinary, which in the one moment elates and moves us only to be replaced in the next moment by the everyday and drab perception of reality has, for some people, been the cause of deep wonder – and for others, the source of a deep sense of longing. Wonder and longing have been basic motives for reflecting upon, exploring and considering what the truth about humanity, its origin, expression and reality creation basically *is*.

Generally, when researchers speak nowadays of exploring and coming to understand humanity, it is mainly a question of science and knowledge about the human genome and the brain functions. Psychological research that takes its point of departure in knowledge about our biological make-up – the genes and the brain functions – is ascribed increasing significance and interest vis-à-vis research. Currently, considerable emphasis is placed on research methods whereby the interaction between brain functions and the human mental and emotional functions and behavior is subjected to external observation.

Both methods of perception – human beings as aware, knowing, sensing, feeling, experiencing, and realizing beings; and human beings as equipped with genetic predispositions and a dynamic brain function that supports the human mental and emotional processes and behavior – give forth their own respective versions of an understanding of humanity. Apparently, these two perspectives of exploration belong to two separate worlds. This becomes evident when witnessing the current polarization and rational bypassing that takes place when scientific legitimacy is conferred on methods of observing phenomena from the outside while introspective and phenomenological methods of exploration are considered private, subjective and lacking in scientific validity. Nonetheless, both methods of exploration involve vital aspects of the functioning of the human mind – present and operational at any moment and in every single human being.

In the following, we will be taking a closer look at how we, as human beings, are capable of bringing about a climate of cooperation between these seemingly irreconcilable aspects. Taking our point of departure in "the ethical paradox", what will briefly be outlined in what follows is how this paradox can be explored in these two distinct approaches of exploration. It will be rendered probable that knowledge from *both* points of departure can be beneficial to our understanding of how seemingly innate obstacles to being caring and considerate toward others can be overcome by consciously working on maturing innate qualities and by expressing our natural ability to be empathic human beings.

The Ethical Paradox and Existential Considerations

As described in Chapter 3, the experience of value is crucial to our experience of meaning and of basic sanity. Adhering to values that make sense is a precondition for us to distinguish between good and evil, between right and wrong, and between true and false. With this in mind, we are able to make choices and decisions and act to the benefit of ourselves and others. This, however, does not mean that we always choose to do so. This is expressed in the ethical paradox: "For I don't do the good I want; instead, the evil that I don't want is what I do."

The individual's existential quest and the formation of philosophical schools, traditions of wisdom, and religions can be viewed as attempts to explore and gain insight into basic aspects of existence. The motives that lie behind this exploration range from wonder at the apparent contradiction between the potential possibilities and the lived reality and to feelings of dissatisfaction and a sense of lack of fulfillment in life. For some, the driving force is a longing to become inseparable from what momentarily and beyond apparent reality is realized as being true. That we have this inclination at all has led, in various cultures throughout the history of humanity, to insight into what can be formulated as a universal "source" of existence beyond and untouched by human notions, thoughts and actions.

Some traditions take their point of departure in insights into an inconceivable absolute truth, from which everything unfurls, while others – for example, theistic traditions – perceive truth as an omnipresent creator, God. However, whether we are dealing with secular or religious approaches, there is evidence that an open present awareness that is free from conceptualization and habitual thought patterns intensifies an experience of being connected with what is felt to be authentic and true.

In the thousands of years in which there is evidence that we, as human beings, have been occupied by comprehensively exploring the nature of humanity, consciousness and existence, it is indeed striking to observe how very similar the motives for undertaking these explorations have been and how similar the experiences and the insight that have been obtained in the process appear to be. This is so regardless of whether the exploration has been conducted on the basis of a secular philosophical outlook, a spiritual view or a religious faith. [126]

Present awareness, reflection, introspection, contemplation and meditation have proved themselves to be crucial to our ability to cut through the mental thought structures and habitual emotional patterns of conventional reality. A direct experience of the nature of reality and existence can be achieved through some of these practices. Having such an experience is not reserved exclusively to practitioners of specific philosophical, spiritual or religious movements. We might say that no faith or philosophical school can lay claim to being the only approach to mobiliz-

---

[126] To be mentioned in this connection are, e.g., the Greek philosopher Plotinus, the Catholic Meister Eckhart, Jajal al-Din Rumi of the Muslim Sufi tradition, Moshe ben Shem-Tov de León of the Jewish kabbalah tradition, the Upanishads of Hinduism, Taoism as represented by Lau Tsu and the collection of texts knows as Tao The Ching, as well as modern contemplative Christians like Thomas Merton and Thomas Keating.

ing our inherent ability to acquire insight into, reflect on, and experience the nature of mind and existence. Having said this some traditions - i.e. Buddhist philosophic schools - more than others aim at and have developed methods in order to analyze and directly experience the nature of mind.

The great world religions, including, for instance, theistic Judaism, Christianity, Islam, and Hinduism, and the non-theistic philosophical spiritual movements like Buddhism and Taoism, as well as certain European-based philosophical schools have, in the course of time, each developed traditions of wisdom. The study of philosophical texts, the exploration of outer reality, and the collection of data have been conducted alongside the practicing of reflection, introspection, contemplation and meditation. The introspective and contemplative methods have been employed when human beings have wanted to acquire knowledge about aspects of existence that we cannot attain through rational thought or explore through the observation of the outer world.

If we look at the descriptions of direct experience obtained by methods like introspection, contemplation and meditation, we can see that there is a remarkable degree of consensus between the various philosophies and schools of wisdom on significant points: 1) the notion of the self as an isolated, static and delimited entity gradually gives way to the experiencing of an ever increasing degree of unsolidified being-in-aware-presence; 2) the true nature of reality is experienced as a timeless and multidimensional unfolding of qualities such as love, wisdom, will, strength, power, joy, peace and harmony. An intensified sense of reality lying beyond conceptualization and the concurrent experience of the indisputable truth of what is being experienced are the perspectives from which the everyday perception of reality is acknowledged as being limited and distorted. [127]

What is usually perceived as reality is, according to this insight, conditioned by the concepts and opinions that we form about reality while being in a state of ignorance about the true state of existence. According to the teachings of Mahayana Buddhism, this conditioned reality is illu-

---

[127] When a person, in glimpses, perceives the true nature, this corresponds, according to Mahayana Buddhism, to seeing an image of the moon in a lake. It is a clear representation, indeed, but it is not the moon itself. A person who has realized the true nature, including acknowledging the dependent existence of self and of phenomena and of their empty nature, will only reluctantly attempt to denote and put into words what can be known but not described. It is thus with a point of departure in ordinary thought that an approximation of ultimate truth can be presented. See Norbu, 2006 and Mipham, 2004.

sory and yet it appears: we experience it, form concepts about it and act on it. An analytical distinction is drawn between the conventional or relative reality and absolute truth. From the point of view of relative reality, phenomena and objects are experienced as isolated from each other. At the same time, relations between the phenomena of the relative world are perceived as mutually interdependent, that is, they are viewed as being the causes, conditions and effects of each other, in processes that unfold in a temporal perspective of past, present and future. This is how we, as human beings, who are ignorant of absolute truth, experience and create the infinitely varied personal and collective stories that unfold in life's cycles of birth, life, decay and death. [128]

The insight into and gradual realization of the true nature is expressed as ever higher degrees of mental clarity, attentive empathic presence and emotional balance. The person increasingly thinks and acts selflessly and altruistically and expresses real and authentic human qualities. Regardless of whether the person adheres to a specific philosophy or a religious faith or holds a secular view of life, he or she will inspire others to feel a reflection of their own human potentials and qualities.

Different causes for the separation

Even if the different wisdom-espousing traditions and religious beliefs display similarities with regard to experiences of what seems to be truth, there are crucial differences that can be spotted when it comes to establishing the cause of humanity's separation from this truth.

In the Judeo-Christian religious tradition, in which humanity is thought to have been created by God and in God's image, there is a notion of a fall – the Fall of Man – out of the union with God. Metaphorically, according to the legend of Creation, this happened when the first human being in Paradise sinned against God by taking a bite of the apple from the Tree of Knowledge. This sin – the original sin – cast humanity out from the paradisiac state of union with God and of being in harmony with all of God's creation. In the ensuing dual state, there exists a polarity between I and you, between good and evil, between right and wrong, and between true and false. Humanity's path toward reuniting with God moves through repentance and calling upon oneself to live in accordance with the laws lain down by God. In the Christian tradition, which shares the Old Testament with Judaism, Jesus Christ is portrayed, in the New Testament, as the Son of God. The faith in Christ as the savior, who

---

[128] There seems to be an interesting similarity between Mahayana Buddhism and the thinking espoused by physicist Werner Heisenberg inasmuch as he makes a careful distinction between what appears – and what is measured in the physical world – and the essential nature of the physical phenomena

redeems us from sin, is central to a Christian person's reunification with God.

In Buddhism, it is *ignorance* that is regarded as the cause of humanity's separation from true being. The true nature is considered to be inherent in everything there is and in everything which appears to us. It is accordingly not a state beyond this world. Ignorance did not come into being once upon a time, but comes into being at every instant, we are not aware of our true nature. According to Buddha Shakyamuni, who realized this insight 2600 years ago in India, ignorance occurs when resting with awareness in the true nature, time and time again, is replaced by lack of awareness. This being repeated, a more and more fixed and habitual view of existence that is being experienced from an ignorant perspective takes place. Being ignorant, "I" is perceived as being separate from "other" and from the surrounding reality. The dual mode of perception and the inherent fear and inadequacy (suffering) that are due to ignorance and being separated from true nature lie at the heart of the struggle to secure "I" and to repel what is experienced as being a threat to the "I". It is thus in the state of ignorance that human beings form concepts, notions and thoughts about the self and the other. An increasing urge to being attracted to and desiring whatever appears to be beneficial and the urge to avert and fight off whatever is perceived as being threatening to self-preservation are the driving forces in further developing a distorted view of self and reality.

From the Buddhist perspective human suffering is caused by the fact that human beings strive in vain to consolidate their own illusory existence and hence to achieve (lasting) happiness, while at the same time they have to fight whatever seems to obstruct this. Emotional states such as desire, hate, indifference (ignorance), jealousy and pride, as well as the endless variations hereof, are expressed in the interactions between ignorant people and their surroundings.

Thus, in Buddhism, it is not faith but self-experienced insights and knowledge that liberate humanity from ignorance and the distorted perception of self and existence. This takes place through the study of philosophical texts and through logical reasoning, reflection, introspection, analytical meditation and contemplation. In meditative attentiveness, the stream of distorted thoughts and emotions abates, whereby the individual, in the ensuing moments of attentive presence, can experience and realize what can be known as truth beyond conceptualization. Something similar is practiced within religions' traditions, for example, inside monasteries as well as within traditions arising from philosophical wisdom, where the faculty of introspection, contemplation and meditation is applied.

By making an effort to consciously train one's capacity to be present and mindful in daily life, ethical discernment is developed as well as the ability to be empathic and to act with compassion. Hereby, the individual will gradually come to know his or her own qualities and will express them according to what is needed in the situation. The distorted perception of reality and the habitual thought structures are gradually dissipated and replaced by what is experienced as being authentic and true.

The ethical paradox and biological preconditions

In the following, we will take a closer look at humanity's biological make-up and functioning. From this perspective we, as human beings, are supposedly conditioned by our instincts and drives, which are an integral part of our biological make-up and which are preconditions contributing to the survival of the individual and the species. [129] However, as opposed to most animals, we are not characterized by being irretrievably tied to and controlled by instincts and drives in the sense that they are automatically expressed as specifically non-learned behavior. Through the course of human history, in the progressive process of our development and maturation, we have sought to achieve command of these lower functions by way of mobilizing higher human potentials in order to consciously control and chose how these instincts and drives will be expressed. Furthermore, from the time of forming communities, human beings appear to have reflected upon and acknowledged the necessity of consciously developing and refining socially responsible behavior.

Throughout the history of man, there is evidence that we have instigated common norms and frames of references that demarcate what are thought of as appropriate attitudes and ways of behavior. (5) In all known societies up until today, norms, laws and rules that regulate human thought, attitudes and behavior have been established so that the individual and the community will act as beneficially as possible and in the least harmful manner. This strategy of regulation gets passed on during the socialization process from one generation to the next, in accordance with the culture that is prevailing at any given time. One very concrete and everyday example is the taking part in communal meals and in the norms surrounding this activity. This was instigated in the very early stages of the formation of communities.

---

129 As we will try later on to juxtapose the biological understanding with, e.g., a Buddhist understanding, it ought to be stressed here that the biological approach is situated, according to the Buddhist Madhyamika philosophy, at the level of "relative reality". Theories on this level spring from the way that reality is conventionally experienced and described.

When we are faced with an ethical paradox, it is because – when we view it from the biological perspective – taking care of ourselves as the first and foremost matter of concern is deeply ingrained in us and is connected to our survival instincts. Thereby we secure the fulfillment of our own needs before securing those of anybody else and, at times, at the expense of others. One important aspect of developing and maturing as a human being is accordingly learning to distinguish between actually being in mortal danger if our needs are not being met here and now and other situations where we can be confident that there is what it takes for ourselves and others around us to survive. A further maturation occurs when we experience that gratification can be postponed without perishing, just as it can be a source of joy to let others have their needs satisfied before we ourselves partake of our share.

Another crucial aspect of our biological make-up and functioning is experiencing the feeling of pleasure that is related to having one's needs fulfilled and experiencing the pain related to unfulfilled needs. In both cases, the expectation of, respectively, pleasure enjoyed in connection with gratification and escalating pain linked with an unfulfilled need are important driving forces that can take control of our attitudes and behavior. When these experiences are stored in the memory, habitual patterns that tend to be self-igniting when triggered by repetition are formed. At the same time, neural networks in the brain are supposedly formed that are similarly reinforced by repetition. Thereby, a mutual reinforcement of attitudes and behavior and of brain function occurs.

Letting go of habitual patterns related to the gratification of needs and drives can be extremely difficult even when we really want to let go. This is due to a basic fear of being or feeling threatened with the loss of one's life when the gratification of needs and drives is not obtained and it is also the manifestation of an equally basic urge to achieve pleasure and avoid pain. In instances when the drive is not fulfilled, instinctual and fear-based survival mechanisms may go so far as to activate aggression in order to achieve gratification and avoid despair or resignation. It is thus literally a matter of age-old and utterly basic tendencies in us that we are facing – and that we are often are at odds with – when we wish to gain command over and control these drives and needs in order to provide and share the means of sustenance among everybody in our social community.[130]

---

130 See Mithen, 1996

The common ground of the existential and the biological perspectives

We have hitherto been dealing with two different approaches to understanding humanity: an existential approach and a biological approach. Both of these operate with certain aspects of human beingness that can be called, on the one hand, higher mental and emotional functions which are uniquely human and, on the other, lower primitive functions that we share in common with animals.

Regardless of whether we choose a biological perspective of exploration or an existential perspective, the quest to solve the ethical paradox thus seems to depend on a conscious choice to cultivate higher mental and emotional qualities and to be guided by empathy and care for oneself as well as for others. It is also clear that the phenomena that are subject to exploration employing either of the two perspectives constitutes a reality to the individual, just as knowledge from *both* perspectives can be helpful in understanding human functions, development, thoughts and actions. Whether we tend toward the one or the other perspective or whether we avail ourselves of a combination of both, the individual who wants to live in accordance with his or her ethical values has to be prepared to consciously work on this. [131]

Reflections on how difficult it can be to do what we actually want to do and how difficult it can be to refrain from doing what we do not want to do thus underscore that minimizing self-absorption and self-interest and overcoming the impulse to gratify one's own needs, drives and desires at the expense of others are lifelong processes. It is crucial to us, as human beings – whether we take our point of departure in an existential or in a biological perspective – that we be able to distinguish and make choices that are guided by intelligent judgment and empathy. It is possible to do this if we step out of oblivion and ignorance about who we are and what we are actually capable of as human beings.

Overcoming the battle of survival: an account

In the following, an account is given about how the biological urge of survival and the self-absorbed tendencies associated with taking care of oneself at the expense of others were overcome by a person who was being held hostage and facing the imminent danger of death from starvation and physical brutality.

---

[131] This view is supported by recent findings that show that not only brain activity but also genes can be activated or remain dormant depending on the development and the conditions of the life of the individual

In her book about her many years of captivity as a hostage in the Columbian jungle, Ingrid Betancourt describes how conflicting groups were formed among the hostages who were facing constant mortal danger. These groups each reflected strategies for managing how to subsist in a constant life-threatening situation. Those of us who have not undergone such an experience over a prolonged duration of time might expect that the hostages would stick together in defiance of the common enemy and try to help and protect each other. But this was far from the case. To Betancourt herself, the vigil became one long uphill struggle to hold tightly onto her own clarity and integrity and to be true to herself and her values when relating to her fellow hostages and the hostage-takers. Furthermore, she had to work hard in order to maintain control over her survival instincts and fears, which came to manifest themselves in situations when she – in cutthroat competition with the other hostages over extremely sparse and arbitrarily administered rations – was forced to realize that she was in the process of gaining access to food as well as other privileges and vital goods at the expense of the other hostages.

Betancourt's account is exemplary in that she, in the course of events, achieved the freedom and peace that set in when she gave up viewing survival as a struggle. When she found meaning and value in – regardless of the conditions – being in tune with what was precious to her as a person and fellow human being. From this point onwards, she was no longer afraid of living the life as a hostage or of being permanently in imminent danger of dying. [132]

The ethical paradox on a societal level

In the following, we will examine why it is apparently extremely difficult for us, as individual citizens, managers and employees, to offer resistance to the prevailing way of thought and rhetoric, even if we are basically and sincerely opposed to it.

The unique potential of human beings is not a concern for the neoliberal societies unless these potentials happen to serve specific interests in the maintenance and consolidation of the growth and profit maximization of the market. This crucially influences the way in which national states, in cooperation with financial capital, production enterprises and public institutions manage, organize and control the market and the citizens of society. The regulation of allegedly "primitive" human instincts

---
[132] Betancourt, 2011

and drives has been placed outside the citizens' domain, in the form of plans for development and learning that follow the individual from childhood and as long as he or she displays the ability to work.

In times of financial crises, the fear of losing one's job and the fear of being left without being able to justify one's existence in society, however, will become concrete and imminent threats. This can give rise to an even more pronounced tendency toward fear-based submission. More or less conscious of the increasing and underlying fear, we, as citizens, are prone to being caught and manipulated into a way of thinking and way of behaving that conforms to the control and management strategies we are being subjected to. As conformists and socially adapted citizens, we contribute to maintaining the prevailing social system at all costs. Whether we want to or not, we will inevitably be corroborating the assumptions that incessant growth and competition constitute the "natural order" and that competition is a (vital) necessity. We will furthermore be subscribing to the belief that progressive growth is achieved by ruthlessly exploiting nature and human beings. As producers – who are subject to the over-taxation of our capacity to work – and as over-consuming customers, we contribute to cementing the doctrine about the necessity of achieving success by participating in the race for goods. [133]

Initially, we as citizens might feel an impulse to choose to integrate ourselves into the prevailing understanding of society and perception of reality – firmly buttressed by, among other things, fear-based attitude regulations and the latest strict management strategies and methods of control and evaluation. By seeing ourselves as active and responsible participants and producers who are contributing to the success of growth in society, we can, for some period of time, avoid having to come to grips with the democratic deficit, with the feeling of having lost influence and with the reality of being powerless.

Without real influence citizens become willing agents who in blatant competition with each other support the selection mechanism that maintains the societal elimination race between those who are fit and benefit from competition, and those who fail and are the losers in the competition

Sacrificing our capacity for reflection and self-reflection, which concomitantly results in a lacking impulse on our part to discern whether we – from an overarching perspective as well as in the concrete reality

---

[133] When totalitarian forces take over a society, parallels can be observed regarding the way in which the citizens are likely to react.

of everyday life – are living in accordance with personal attitudes and values is perhaps the highest price we, as citizens, are taking upon ourselves to pay.

The dehumanization and incapacitation of human beings – and the tendency toward totalizing citizens in a democratic society – is, from the outset and as a result, devastating. Added to this is the fact that the resulting, escalating and cynical subversion and impoverishment of human beings is not only meaningless but also completely unnecessary – something that should never have taken place.

Perhaps we have finally reached a point at which we are ready to unveil what it is that has brought us to the current state of affairs. A point at which we openly and honestly acknowledge that we have been deceived and seduced by a fearful urge to secure our self-interest and simultaneously have tried to deny who we are and what we are capable of. That we have surrendered to powerful forces that likewise have succeeded, out of self-interest, to convince us – with power and with cynicism – that we, by succumbing to our roles in a pathetic game that cannot be won, will get our share of the loot. Perhaps, when we dare to see ourselves honestly and with empathy for ourselves and each other, we will have the courage, the will, and the power to acknowledge our self-deception and start working on making the necessary and considerable changes in ourselves and in the world.

Paradigm shift: investigating reality

The term "paradigm shift" has chiefly been used to denote important new departures within the natural sciences. [134] The limitations of conventional thinking have been overcome while new ways of description and new linguistic formulations have gained a footing. It is thus no longer a necessary condition that linguistic statements about the object of investigation be formulated in accordance with what makes sense from the point of view of conventional language usage.

Not only has this paradigm shift caused a gigantic expansion in the way we acquire knowledge; it has also opened up the field of what can be known. Different theories that were previously thought to be mutually exclusive now exist side by side and are regarded as complementary. Atoms take on the dimension of universes and to the Universe itself are

---

[134] Kuhn, 1962. The concept of "paradigm shift" was introduced by the American philosopher of science, Thomas Kuhn.

added more and more dimensions and universes. The mutual relations of exchange among spaces of existence seem to occur in multidimensional fields that can be roughly elucidated by abstract and complex mathematical models and calculations. Energy and particles arise out of a void and are so transient that "they" – in much the manner of black matter and black energy, which supposedly exist everywhere in the universe – can only be registered by virtue of the influence they exert in relation to other phenomena. Research is dealing, in other words, with phenomena about whose existence something can be inferred but not observed and which can be known and communicated about.

In recent years, an apparent congruity among linguistic expressions has been observed, on the one hand, in intensive studies of consciousness conducted for hundreds of years within the realm of Mahyana and Vajrayana Buddhism and, on the other, in the exploration of physical phenomena transpiring within the field of astrophysics. Within both these respective areas, we can find the statement: "out of a void or of emptiness, a "self-arising" of phenomena takes place". This is put forth without any explicit indication that Buddhism and astrophysics are talking about the same thing. [135]

If we look at research and theories that are flourishing within the social sciences and the humanities and at research being carried out at the juncture between medicine, sociology, psychology, and neuroscientific brain and consciousness research, it is remarkable that these research areas appear to be only sparsely influenced by paradigm shifts within the natural sciences. The prevalent pre-scientific assumptions, theories and methods seem to be virtually unaffected by the enormous expansion of the research field and view of reality that has taken place within natural science.

The concept of objectivity and the assumption that only what can be observed and registered externally and assessed quantitatively are still dominant criteria within scientific exploration. As a consequence, the research that is being conducted that complies with fulfilling the aforementioned criteria accordingly attracts the most funds, affording it a preeminent position when weighed against other methods of exploration. Thus, qualitative research that applies phenomenological methods like introspection, reflection and self-reflection and where the data contain subjective statements is not afforded the same scientific legitimacy and does not attract the same amount of funding. Hence these studies appear to be insignificant.

---

[135] Richard & Thuan, 2001

For a paradigm shift to happen, the predominance of this rational bypassing has to be supplanted with recognition of the complementarity of objective and subjective methods of exploration. The absurdity of making a distinction between objectivity and subjectivity in the exploration of modes of functioning and behavior appears to be especially conspicuous within the neuroscientific exploration of consciousness. Consciousness is claimed as originating from the activity that takes place in the enormously complex networks of the brain. In the name of objectivity, it is claimed, furthermore, that it is the brain which is the origin of our thinking, feeling and making sense and that the cause of mental and emotional activity is to be found in the activation of specific regions of the brain. It does not seem to matter that taking this point of departure is founded on the tacit assumption of a "first cause" that is situated in the brain – an assumption that can never be substantiated.

Exploration of the multi-faceted mind

The scientific exploration of and knowledge about consciousness is currently very limited. It might show to be of significance that an emphasis within some areas in the field of neuroscience has been focused on studying the functioning of mind from "within". In the field of exploration of the relationship between brain function and human consciousness studies are conducted in universities of the U.S.A. addressed toward determining whether Buddhist meditation can contribute to a further understanding of the relationship of the formation and functioning of the brain and the formation and functioning of consciousness. [136] This research could open up for completely new perspectives, eventually affording more comprehensive insight into how the brain and consciousness and the human potential is best matured and expressed.

From several cultures, and at different points in the history of mankind, we have testimonies to the fact that contemplative research, which makes use of strict logical reasoning and minute introspective studies, has led to altogether unique insights and knowledge about human consciousness and the functioning of the mind: knowledge that can be tested by anyone who wishes to do so, under controlled conditions and under the expert guidance of persons who have acquired and integrated the relevant methods themselves. Through what are initially simple and then gradually more complex methods, it has been possible to expand knowledge about the mind and to experience and realize, in the course of the process, what can be called the true nature of mind and existence. These studies have been undertaken for the sole purpose of acquiring

---

[136] Wallace, 2012; Davidson, 2000

knowledge and eventually realizing humanity's authentic qualities and expressing these to the benefit of everybody. [137]

We are dealing with procedures which, from the very outset, have the following features in common: 1) the ability of consciousness to focus – for instance, on a sound, on an object, on a notion or on the breath. By maintaining such a focus, the attention that we ordinarily invest in thoughts and emotional states – and that constantly arises in our mind – is gradually diminished. Mental and emotional activity abates and a state of relaxation and inner calm is attained. 2) When one's conscious focus on an object, an image or the breath, in this state of calm and relaxation, is released and consciousness rests in this state, a shift in the level of consciousness may occur. Insights that cannot be thought up by the mind but which can be grasped and subsequently verbalized may occur. These experiences of insight can be exchanged and validated by others who are familiar with this kind of insight meditation themselves. It is also from relaxed states of mind that creativity, inventive thinking and innovation unfold. Deeper states of insight may also open up for experiencing and knowing human qualities and values. Moreover, it is possible to spontaneously gain certainty about states of mind and existence which, beyond the shadow of any doubt, are experienced as real and true. Resting in this state is associated with inner clarity – in the state of a serene, pure, and carefree being - in attentive, cognizant and alert presence. The absence of the limitations and worries of the self that is usually experienced in our everyday life is in a timeless space of self-forgetfulness inseparably united with a feeling of deep contentment and true, inner joy - and knowing that everybody and all of existence – irrespective of our being consciously aware this or not – is enveloped in this state. Furthermore a deep wish to share the state of natural unfolding of immense goodness and wisdom arise from the person resting in that state.

As pointed out earlier this has been experienced throughout the human history in various cultural, philosophical and religious traditions. Everyone is at liberty, whether he/she claims to be an atheist or professes allegiance to a religious faith or subscribes to some particular spiritual attitude or belief, to use his/her own capacity of mind for self-exploration and to apply relevant methods to this end. On its part, this may foster a gradual transcendence from the ignorant – or, if you like, the bio-

---

[137] There is proof that this contemplative science was being carried out in Asia and the Near Orient several centuries before the Common Era and that it has been continued up until our time. Historical sources from, e.g., Hinduism, Taoism, Buddhism, philosophical schools, and Jewish, Christian and Muslim contemplative traditions show that these studies and methods have been applied under very different historical and cultural circumstances.

logically conditioned – self-indulgent circling around fear-based survival thinking and behavior. Hedonistic self-interest and the urge to acquire the fleeting and potentially addictive experience of pleasure through the gratification of needs and drives will also be weakened, gradually.

The more we are able to transcend the primitive functions so that these no longer determine our view of existence and self-expression, the more we will get to know ourselves through the unfolding of authentic human qualities that we share freely with others. Liberation from the devastation of being dehumanized and alienated from our unique human potentials and from the underlying agenda's illusory straightjacket everywhere we face it is made possible when this underlying agenda is defused and discharged. It is in the realization of the priceless, our true being, that we have the courage and clarity to reject the rational bypassing and its fatal reduction and alienation of humanity.

Seeing the extraordinary in the ordinary

Unlike the straightforward documentation, a work of art holds, almost hidden and unnoticeable, a luminous glow which transcends the reality that the work of art depicts. A picture, a poem, or a piece of music that displays the mere horror of existence is nothing but a lifeless piece of plagiarism, a caricature, if it does not hold a color, a sentence or a sequence of sound that points beyond the depiction of the work. So that we, while steeped in horror, sense and recognize the inextinguishable glow which, in that instant, unites us with the very lifeblood and essence of the work of art and with our own existence.

We are incessantly undergoing a process of becoming as human beings. Mutable, moving and present everywhere and in everything that is held by our Mind. Whenever and wherever we happen to be open and in a state of attentive, aware presence, we have the potential to be illuminated by the wordless that can be known but cannot be named. It is in that instant, in the golden moment of being self-forgetfully present, that we transcend the illusory depiction and that we realize, in a flash, who we truly are. Just as we have seen and realized so often, so fleetingly – and have forgotten it again.

In the first chapter of the book, reflection on the following three questions was suggested:

1. What will the handling of current crises and the prevention of coming disasters demand of us?

2. What will it take for us to deal with the extensive changes we are going to have to accept?

3. How can we, as human beings, muster what it takes to create completely new and sustainable conditions for life in a global era?

It is up to every one of us to create space and time for reflection on these questions and to consciously consider the pressing challenges of the times. To become engaged in reflections that can motivate us to create decisive new departures whereby we, as human beings, individually and collectively, can break free from destructive and unnecessary limitations. Not only because it is a matter of survival but also because we – acknowledging our enormous human potentials and qualities – are confident that nothing is more meaningful and mutually enriching than creating decent conditions of life for everybody.

The challenge of humanity in our time is *to see the extraordinary in the ordinary* – in the generosity of the daily empathic presence, which imperceptibly and without cause arises in the exchange between human beings as an unconditional and mutual affirmation of being human.

Bibliography

Acemoglu, D. & J. Robinson (2011). *Why Nations Fail. The Origin of Power, Prosperity and Poverty.* London: Profile Books.

Ahrensbach, L.; S. H. Petersen; U. Østergaard & M.G. Haaning (2012). "Mast under bundlinjen". *Psykolog Nyt*, May 18.

Ainsworth, Mary D. Salter, et al. (1962). *Deprivation of Maternal Care: A Reassessment of its Effects.* Geneva: WHO.

Akerlof, G. & R. Kranton (2010). *Identity Economics.* New Jersey: Princeton University Press.

Almaas, A. H. (2000). *The Pearl Beyond Price – Integration of Personality into Being: An Object Relations Approach.* Boston: Shambhala Publications.

Andersen, Lisbeth Zornig (2011). *Zornig – vrede er mit mellemnavn.* Copenhagen: Gyldendal.

Andersen, L.O.; M.H. Claesson; A. Hróbjartsson & A.N. Sørensen (1997). *Placebo. Historie, biologi og effekt.* Copenhagen: Akademisk Forlag.

Andersen, M.F., Nielsen, K. M. & Brinkmann, S. (2012). "Meta-synthesis of qualitative research on return to work among employees with common mental disorder". *Scandinavian Journal of Work, Environment & Health* vol. 38, n° 2.

Andersen, M.F., Nielsen, K.M., & Brinkmann, S. (2014). "How do Workers with Common Mental Disorder Experience a Multidisciplinary Return-to-Work Intervention? A Qualitative Study". *Journal of Occupational Rehabilitation.* DOI 10, 1007/s10926-014-9498-5

Antonovsky A. (1979). *Health, Stress and Coping.* San Francisco: Jossey-Bass.

Arendt, Hannah (1978). *The Life of the Mind.* New York: Harcourt Brace Jovanovich.

Arendt, Hannah (1958). *The Origins of Totalitarianism.* **New York: Schocken Books.**

d'Arcais, P. F. (2014). Un'altra democrazia per un'altra Europa. *MocroMega 3/2014*, Rome, Italy.

Betancourt, Ingrid (2010). *Even Silence has an End: My Six Years of Captivity.* London: Virago Press

Bohm, D. & D. Peat (1987). *Science, Order, and Creativity.* New York: Bantam Books.

Bohm, D. (1980). *Wholeness and the Implicate Order.* **London: Routledge.**

Bohr, N. (1958). Atomic Physics and Human Knowledge. New York: John Wiley.

Bostrom, N. (2012). Existential Risk Prevention as Global Priority. *Global Policy*, Vol. 4, Issue 1 (2013): pp. 15-31.

Bowlby, J. (1951). *Maternal Care and Mental Health.* **Geneva: WHO.**

Bowlby, J. (1988). *A Secure Base: Clinical Applications of Attachment Theory.* **London: Routledge.**

Buber, M. (2004). *I and Thou.* London: Continuum.

Byrnit, J. (2007). *Mennesket, det hypersociale dyr.* Copenhagen: Dansk Psykologisk Forlag.

Carroll, Roz. "An Interview with Allan Schore – "the American Bowlby". *Thinking Through The Body* http://www.thinkbody.co.uk/papers/interview-with-allan-s.htm, retrieved September 20, 2012.

Christiansen, Sofus (1975). "Subsistence on Bellona Island (Mungiki). A study of a Polynesian Outlier in the British Solomon Islands Protectorate. Annex med 12 kort-plancher". *Folia Geographica Danica*, XIII.

Daly, H. (2009). *Nødvendighedens økonomi*. Gjern: Hovedland.

Davidson, Richard J. (ed.) (2000). *Anxiety, Depression, and Emotion*. New York: Oxford University Press.

Davidson, Richard J. & Anne Harrington (eds.) (2001). *Visions of Compassion: Western Scientists and Tibetan Buddhists Examine Human Nature*. New York: Oxford University Press.

Deacon, Terrence (1997). *The Symbolic Species. The co-evolution of language and the human brain.* New York: W.W. Norton & Company Ltd.

Einstein, A. & L. Infeld (1938). The Evolution of Physics. New York: Simon & Schuster.

Ferrie, J. E. (Ed.) (2004). WORK STRESS AND HEALTH: the Whitehall II Study. International Centre for Health and Society/Department of Epidemiology and Public Health, University College London, United Kingdom.

Fonagy, P., G. Gergely, E.L. Jurist & M. Target (2002). Affect Regulation, Mentalization and the Development of the Self. New York: Other Press.

Foucault, Michel (1988). *The History of Sexuality, Vol. 3: The Care of the Self.* New York: Vintage.

Frank, Robert (2011). *The Darwin Economy. Liberty, Competition and the Common Good.* New Jersey: Princeton University Press.

Frankl, Victor E. (2004). *Man's Search for Meaning*. London: Ebury Press.

Fukuyama, F. (2014). *Political Order and Political Decay.* New York: Farrar, Straus and Goroux.

Gadamer, H.G. (2004). *Truth and Method.* New York: Crossroad.

Gardner, H.; M. Csikszentmihalyi & W. Damon (2001). *Good Work – Where Excellence and Ethics Meet.* New York: Basic Books.

Goldberg, D and I. Goodyer (2005). *The Origins and Cause of Common Mental Disorders.* New York: Routledge.

Habermas, J. (1972). *Knowledge and Human Interests.* Boston: Beacon Press.

Habermas, J. (1987). *Theory of Communicative Action Volume Two: Lifeworld and System: A Critique of Functionalist Reason.* Boston: Beacon Press.

Harlow, H.F. (1958) The Nature of Love. *American Psychologist, 13*, pp. 673-685.

Hart, S. (2006). *Hjerne, samhørighed, personlighed. Introduktion til neuroaffktiv udvikling.* Copenhagen: Hans Reitzels Forlag

Havel, V. (1991), *Disturbing the Peace.* UK, Vintage Books

Harvey, D. (2014). *Seventeen Contradictions and the End of Capitalism.* London: Profile Books.

Heisenberg, Werner (1986). *The Physicist's Conception of Nature.* London: Hutchinson Publishing Group.

Held, D. (2010). *Cosmopolitanism: Ideals and Realities.* London: Wiley.

Hickel, J. (2012). "A Short History of Neoliberalism (and How We Can Fix It)". *New Left Project*, April.

Hickel, J. & K. Arsalan (2012). "The Culture of Capitalism and the Crisis of Critique". *Anthropological Quarterly 85*(1), pp. 203-227.

Honneth, Axel (2008). *Reification: A New Look at an Old Idea.* Oxford: Oxford University Press.

Houshmand, Z.; R.B. Livingston & B.A. Wallace (eds.) (1999). *Consciousness at the Crossroads.* Ithaca, New York: Snow Lion Publications.

Husserl, E. (1962). *Ideas: General Introduction to Pure Phenomenology.* Collins Books, New York.

Høgelund, J. (2012). *Effekter af den beskaeftigelsesrettede indsats for sygemeldte. En litteraturoversigt.* Copenhagen: SFI.

Israel, J. (1972). "Stipulations and Construction in the Social Sciences", in: Joachim Israel and Henri Tajfel (Eds.) *The Context of Social Psychology: A Critical Assessment.* New York: Academic Press.

Israel, J. (1980). *Erkendelse, sprog og sociale relationer: Om kreationistisk socialpsykologi*. Copenhagen: Munksgaard.

Israel, J. (1995). *Martin Buber: Dialogphilophie in Theorie und Praxis*. Berlin: Dunker & Humbolt.

Israel, J (1999). *Handling och samspel: Et socialpsykologisk perspektiv*. Lund: Studentlitteratur.

Israel, S.B. (2011). *Relating People on Film. The Relational Depiction of Human Action and Interaction in Contemporary Multi Protagonist Films as an Approach to Cinematic Storytelling and Why Both Have Largely Been Overlooked*. Ph.D. dissertation, Syddansk Universitet.

Jamgon Kongtrul Lodro Thaye (2007). *Frameworks of Buddhist Philosophy*. Ithaca: Snow Lion Publications.

Jackson, Tim (2009): *Prosperity Without Growth: Economics for a Finite Planet*. New York: Earthscan.

Jaspers, K. (2003). *Way to Wisdom: An Introduction to Philosophy*. New Haven, Connecticut: Yale University Press.

Kaplan, B. (1961). *Studying Personality Cross-Culturally*. New York: Peterson & Comp.

Keepin, W. (1993). *Lifework of David Bohm*. Sebastopol, California: ReVision. 16(1): 32-46.

Kemp, P. (2012). *Filosofiens verden*. Copenhagen: Tiderne Skifter.

Knoop, H.H. (2004). "Om kunsten at finde flow i en verden, der ofte forhindre det". *Kognition og paedagogik*, no. 52. Dansk Psykologisk Forlag, Copenhagen.

Knudsen, T. (2007). *Fra folkestyre til markedsdemokrati. Dansk demokratihistorie efter 1973*. Copenhagen: Akademisk Forlag.

Krugman, P. (2012). *End This Depression Now*. New York: W.W. Norton & Company.

Kuhn, T. (1962). *The Structure of Scientific Revolutions*, 3rd ed., University of Chicago Press.

Kuschel, R. (1977). *Livet i Matahinua, en polynesisk landsby.* Copenhagen: Nationalmuseet.

Køppe, Simo (1990). *Virkelighedens niveauer. De nye videnskaber og deres historie.* Copenhagen: Gyldendal.

Lakoff, G. and M. Johnson (1999). *Philosophy in the Flesh: The Embodied Mind and its Challenge to Western Thought.* New York: Basic Books.

Larsen, N.S. (2008). "Neurovidenskab. En udfordring for filosofisk taenkning". *Gnosis Vedhaeftninger,* no. 2.

Lauritzen, Pia (2011). *Filosofi i ledelse. Vilkår for ledelsesteori og -praksis.* Copenhagen: Hans Reitzels Forlag.

Leach, E.R. (1969). "Virgin birth", in: *Genesis as Myth and other Essays.* London: Cape.

Levine, P. (1997). *Waking the Tiger – Healing Trauma.* Berkeley, California: North Atlantic Books.

Limborg, H.J.; A. Mac; M. Pedersen & O.H. Sørensen (2008). *Arbejdets kerne. Om at arbejde med psykisk arbejdsmiljø i praksis.* Frederiksberg: Frydenlund.

Longchen Rabjampa, Drimé Özer (Longchenpa): Commentary that has been titled: "Thorough Dispelling of Darkness throughout the Ten Directions/Chok Chu", in: *The Guhyagarbha Tantra. Secret Essence Definitive Nature Just As It Is Sangwa'i Nyingpo.* Ithaca, New York: Shambala Publications & Snow Lion (printed in 2011).

Lukács, Georg (1923). *Reification and the Consciousness of the Proletariat* http://www.sfu.ca/~andrewf/books/Reification_Consciousness_Lukacs.pdf

Lund. H.H. (2009). *Mod det todelte samfund – Fra kvalitetsreform til minimumsvelfaerd.* Frederiksberg: Nyt fra samfundsvidenskaberne.

Lund. H.H. (2008). *New Public Management – rehabilitering af markedet. Kritik af markeds-, penge- og profitstyring i det offentlige.* Copenhagen: Alternativ.

Løgstrup, K. E. (1958). *Den etiske fordring.* Copenhagen: Gyldendal.

Mead, M. (1956). *Sex and Temperament in Three primitive Societies*. Dublin: Mentor Books

Meadows, D.H.; D.L. Meadows; J. Randers & W.W. Behrens (1972). The Limits to Growth. New York: Universe Books.

Mears, C. (ed.) (1985). *From Learning to Love. The Selected Papers of H.F. Harlow*. New York: Praeger.

Mipham, J. (2004). *Introduction to the Middle Way. Chandrakirti's Madhyamakavatara with Commentary by Jamgön Mipham*. Boston & London: Shambhala.

Mithen, Steven (1996). *The Prehistory of the Mind. The cognitive origins of art, religion and science*. London: Thames and Hudson.

Monberg, T. (1966). *The Religion of Bellona Island. The Concepts of Supernaturals. Language and Culture of Rennel and Bellona Islands*: Vol. II, part 1. Copenhagen: The National Museum of Denmark.

Monberg, T. (1975): "Fathers were not Genitors". *Man*, vol. 10, no. 1, pp. 34-40.

Nagarjuna (2008): *Root Stanzas on the Middle Way. Mulamadhyamaka-karika*. Chanteloube: Edition Padmakara.

Neufeld, G. & G. Máté (2005). *Hold on to Your Kids. Why Parents Need to Matter More than Peers*. New York: Ballantine Books.

Nielsen, J.S. (2010). *Den store omstilling. Fra systemkrise til grøn økonomi*. Copenhagen: Informations Forlag.

Norbu, Thinley (2006). *A Cascading Waterfall of Nectar*. Boston & London: Shambhala.

Olsen, E. R. (2005). *Syge på tvangsarbejde – om behandlingen af førtidspensionsansøgere*. Copenhagen: Gyldendal.

Penrose, R. (1994). *Shadows of the Mind*. New York: Oxford University Press.

Piketty, T. (2014). *Capital in the Twenty-First Century*. Harvard University Press, Cambridge Massachusetts, United States.

Praetorius, N.U. (1970). *Aggressionsmønstre og deres socialisation på Bellona – et polynesisk ø-samfund*. Copenhagen: Københavns Universitet.

Praetorius-Israel, N.U. & T. Monberg (1971). "Sexuel adfaerd i etnografisk belysning", in: P. Hertoft; H. Hoffmeyer & E. Lykkebo (eds.). *Paedagogisk sexologi, bd. 1*, Copenhagen: Gyldendals Paedagogiske Bibliotek.

Praetorius, N.U. (2002): "Mennesket i produktudviklingens tidsalder" (Man in the Age of Product Development. With a summary in English), in: *Psyke & Logos, 2002 -1: Subjektivitet i det 21. århundrede*. Copenhagen: Dansk Psykologisk Forlag

Praetorius, N. U. (2004): "Livet som undtagelsestilstand. Overlevelsesstrategier, fremmedgørelse og stress set i lyset af styringsstrategier i interpersonelle og samfundsmaessige relationer" (Life as a State of Emergency. Survival Strategies, Alienation and Stress in Interpersonal and Societal Relationships. With a summary in English), in: *Psyke & Logos, 2004 – 2: Temanummer: Dømt til autonomi – Om den ydrestyrede selvforvaltning*. Copenhagen: Dansk Psykologisk Forlag.

Praetorius, N.U.(2007) *Stress – det moderne traume*. Copenhagen: Dansk Psykologisk Forlag.

Praetorius, N.U. (2013). *Den etiske udfordring i en global tid*. Copenhagen: Dansk Psykologisk Forlag.

Praetorius, N.U. (2013). "Stress – et menneskeligt svar på umenneskelige betingelser", in: Andersen, M.F. and S. Brinkmann (eds.). *Nye perspektiver på stress*. Aarhus: Klim

Praetorius, N.U. (2014). "Omstillingens etiske udfordring. Om konkurrencestatens tingsliggørelse, fremmedgørelse og stress", in: Illeris, K (Ed.) *Laering I konkurrencestaten. Kapløb eller baeredygtighed*. Frederiksberg: Samfundslitteratur

Praetorius, N.U. (2014). "Dannelse: Empatisk samarbejde eller fremmedgørende Underkastelse" in: *Kognition og Paedagogik (2014) 24 årgang nr, 94. Temanummer: Etik – Faellesskab – Dannelse*. Copenhagen: Dansk Psykologisk Forlag.

Richard, M. & T.X. Thuan (2001): *The Quantum and the Lotus. A Journey to the Frontiers where Science and Buddhism Meet*. New York: Three Rivers Press.

Rifkin, Jeremy (2010). *The Empathic Civilization: The Race to Global Consciousness in a World in Crisis.* New York: Penguin.

Rifkin, J. (2014) *The Zero Marginal Cost Society: The Internet of Things, the Collaborative Commons, and the Eclipse of Capitalism.* New York: Palgrave Macmillan.

Rutter, M. (2002): "Nature, Nurture, and Development, from Evangelism through Science toward Policy and Practice", in: *Child Development, Vol. 73, issue 1,* New Jersey, Wiley

Schore, A.N. (1994). *Affect Regulation and the Origin of the Self. The Neurobiology of Emotional Development.* Mahwah, New Jersey: Lawrence Erlbaum Associates, Inc., Publishers.

Skjervheim, H. (2000). *Objektivismen – og studiet av mennesket.* Oslo: Gyldendal Akademisk.

Spiro, M.E. (1966). "Religion: Problems of Definition and Explanation", in: M. Banton (ed.). *Anthropological Approaches to the Study of Religion.* London: Tavistock.

Spitz, R.A. (1945). "Hospitalism – An Inquiry Into the Genesis of Psychiatric Conditions in Early Childhood." *Psychoanalytic Study of the Child,* 1, pp. 53-74.

Stansfeld, S. and B. Candy (Eds.) (2006) Psychosocial work environment and mental health – a meta-analytic review. *Scandinavian Journal of Work, Environment & Health* [2006, 32(6): 443-462].

Stiglitz, J. (2012). *The Price of Inequality: How Today's Divided Society Endangers Our Future.* New York: Norton & Company.

Sørensen, J.H.; P. Fornagy; D. Stern & A. Schore (2006). *Affektregulering i udvikling og psykoterapi.* Copenhagen: Hans Reitzels Forlag.

Tsoknyi Rinpoche (2012). *Open Heart, Open Mind. Awakening the Power of Essence Love.* New York: Harmony Books.

Turkle, S. (2011). *Alone Together. Why We Expect More from Technology and Less from Each Other.* New York: Basic Books.

Wallace, B.A. (2006). *Contemplative Science: Where Buddhism and Neuroscience Converge.* New York: Columbia University Press.

Wallace, B.A. (2012). *Meditations of a Buddhist Skeptic: A Manifesto for the Mind Sciences and Contemplative Practice.* New York: Columbia University Press.

Welzer, H. (2011). Mental Infrastructures. How Growth Entered the World and Our Souls. *Heinrich Böll Stiftung, Publication Series on Ecology, Volume 14.*

Whiting, J.W.M., et al. (1966). *Field Guide for a Study of Socialization. Six Culture Series,* vol. I. New York: Wiley.

Willig, R. (2009). *Umyndiggørelse.* Copenhagen: Hans Reitzels Forlag.

Wolin, S. S. (2010). *Democracy Incorporated: Managed Democracy and the Specter of Inverted Totalitarianism.* New Jersey: Princeton University Press.

Wolf, C. (2014): *City of Angels or The Overcoat of Dr. Freud.* New York: Farrar, Strauss and Giroux

About the Author

Nadja U. Praetorius PhD, MA Phil, is an author, Associate professor and specialist in psychology and a supervisor in psychotherapy.

She started her university career as a teacher and researcher and was subsequently employed as associate professor in intercultural psychology and social psychology at the University of Copenhagen and RUC. During the same period she had a research grant at the Sorbonne, Paris, and served as a visiting professor at universities in the United States, where she taught intercultural research.

After several years of university tenure, she chose a career change and went into practice as a clinical psychologist. Basing her work on therapist education in both Scandinavia and the United States, she worked in private practice as well as holding a position as a supervisor and teacher for psychologists and other professionals in private and public institutions. She has been involved specifically in the prevention and treatment of trauma and stress.

In 2007, she published "Stress – The Modern Trauma" and in 2013 "The Ethical Challenge in Global Times". In 2016, she released "Verden til Forskel" (Making a World of Difference) in Denmark.

She has co-authored anthologies about stress and inappropriate working conditions in the social and health services and in educational institutions, (KLIM publishing house and Forlag Samfundslitteratur, Forlaget Jensen and Dalgaard).

Praetorius has also published a wide range of research articles. She lectures by invitation at Universities and University Colleges, abroad and at home, in trade unions and at conferences on working conditions. She is currently researching and co-authoring two forthcoming Academic works on work-ethics.